Librarianship and Human Rights

CHANDOS
INFORMATION PROFESSIONAL SERIES

Series Editor: Ruth Rikowski
(email: Rikowskigr@aol.com)

Chandos' new series of books are aimed at the busy information professional. They have been specially commissioned to provide the reader with an authoritative view of current thinking. They are designed to provide easy-to-read and (most importantly) practical coverage of topics that are of interest to librarians and other information professionals. If you would like a full listing of current and forthcoming titles, please visit our web site **www.chandospublishing.com** or contact Hannah Grace-Williams on email info@chandospublishing.com or telephone number +44 (0) 1865 884447.

New authors: we are always pleased to receive ideas for new titles; if you would like to write a book for Chandos, please contact Dr Glyn Jones on email gjones@chandospublishing.com or telephone number +44 (0) 1865 884447.

Bulk orders: some organisations buy a number of copies of our books. If you are interested in doing this, we would be pleased to discuss a discount. Please contact Hannah Grace-Williams on email info@chandospublishing.com or telephone number +44 (0) 1865 884447.

Librarianship and Human Rights

A twenty-first century guide

TONI SAMEK

Foreword by Edgardo Civallero

With contributions by Kenneth D. Gariepy

Chandos Publishing

Oxford · England

Chandos Publishing (Oxford) Limited
Chandos House
5 & 6 Steadys Lane
Stanton Harcourt
Oxford OX29 5RL
UK
Tel: +44 (0) 1865 884447 Fax: +44 (0) 1865 884448
Email: info@chandospublishing.com
www.chandospublishing.com

First published in Great Britain in 2007

ISBN:
978 1 84334 146 8 (paperback)
978 184334 198 7 (hardback)
1 84334 146 8 (paperback)
1 84334 198 0 (hardback)

British Library Cataloguing-in-Publication Data.
Samek, Toni, 1964–
    Librarianship and human rights: a twenty-first century guide / Toni Samek ; foreword
by Edgardo Civallero ; with contributions by Kenneth D. Gariepy. — 1st ed.
        p. cm.
    Includes bibliographical references and index.
    ISBN   1 84334 198 0
            1 84334 146 8 (pbk.)
    1. Library science—Philosophy. 2. Library science—Moral and ethical aspects. 3.
Human rights. 3. Social action—Handbooks, manuals, etc. 4. Social change—Citizen
participation—Handbooks, manuals, etc. 5. Librarians—Professional ethics. 6.
Libraries and society. I. Gariepy, Kenneth D. (Kenneth Donald), 1970– II. Title.
Z665   020.1

Typeset by Avocet Typeset, Chilton, Aylesbury, Bucks.
Printed in the UK and USA.

This book is dedicated to the many courageous library and information workers throughout the world and through the generations who have taken personal and professional risk to push for social change.

Contents

Foreword

Information means power; economic power as well as social, political and human. This great power has always been seized by a few and it is not often shared.

Since the beginning of time, information has made it possible to understand the pace of nature and to make the most of its resources. It was at the time when the land gave birth to many crops, when the rivers were tamed and their flow was controlled, when stone and adobe were used as building materials to erect walls, pyramids and ziggurats, when we learnt how to treat some diseases and how to shape iron and glass into tools and weapons, that information was consciously kept safe by privileged minorities: shamans, leaders and craft masters.

As cities developed and the basic framework of society became increasingly complex, writing arose as a useful tool for organising work, dealing with surpluses and accumulating wealth. Indeed, it is more than likely that writing was also used to preserve a developing social pyramid for centuries to come. The esteemed scribes managed available human and material resources (for the benefit of the richest people's financial arks), wrote stories (according to the winners' point of view), publicly and officially told people about the importance of castes in charge, expressed admiration for heroes, praised official gods and laid down the rules of Heaven and Earth, i.e. the patterns of behaviour expected in real life as well as in the one after death.

Writing made it possible to preserve learned knowledge for posterity, but at the same time, it also built one of the most devastating barriers for human beings to overcome: illiteracy. An oral tradition continued to exist (and still does); however, most relevant information and strategic knowledge was hidden under the mysterious layer of written symbols. As a consequence, knowing how to write and manage and organise information resulted in having power. Until printing systems were born, information was recorded in strips made from agave fibres by Aztec and Mayan priests, in the codices of papyrus made in European monasteries, in Islamic and Jewish manuscripts, in bamboo tablets from southeastern Asia, or in Chinese bands of silk. The rest continued through talk, passed down from generation to generation. However, the most valuable oral knowledge still remained in the hands of the privileged individuals.

This state of knowledge made possible the improvement of navigation techniques and the development of a modern medicine that resulted in new horizons being discovered inwards and outwards; it also played a leading role in developing many different devices and machines in order to improve industry and agriculture, allowing economic development and growth to take place. However, more efficient weapons were created at the same time. Everything positive has a negative side and no exception should be applied to knowledge.

The invention of printing press set knowledge free. The growing number of books reached thousands of hands making it possible that the pleasure of reading and the opportunity to write increased at the same time. Reading should have meant being able to explain and apprehend new ideas, to have the right and the freedom and to make use of both, to break chains, to loosen gags. But still relevant information was not made available for the majority; it remained in a few educated hands: scientists, philosophers and aristocrats.

The sands of time passed slowly and inexorably through the hourglass of history. The world has been the impassive (though injured) witness that has seen social and industrial revolutions, nonsense wars, astonishing discoveries, hunger and death, diseases and plagues, the mushroom cloud of the atomic bomb and demonstrations supporting peace, defeated monsters and ghosts to be hunted. In one way or another, information has played a crucial role in history's development, and in all cases, this knowledge has always belonged to the very few people who have organised life to suit themselves. Progress, development, 'First World', wealth, health, safety, education, happiness and growth have only benefited a small minority: the majority of people continued to be on the other side of the information, literacy and knowledge divide, hardly maintaining their identities and cultures, struggling to survive in a world that left them behind, and at the very bottom of the organisation.

At present time, information has become a consumer good, the imaginary line around which the current 'knowledge society' draws. Digital revolution and the improvement of telecommunication technologies permit knowledge recovery, storage and management. Quick, direct and constant connectivity with very distant places also provides the chance to carry a library in our pockets on a simple plastic sheet.

However, in spite of those many discoveries, findings and open doors, the particular way of doing things and organising theories and ideas continues to be the same and unfortunately very little has changed. There are still well informed and misinformed people and a widening gap between rich and poor. There are still whole peoples condemned to a life of ignorance and silence. And there are a shameful number of people who do not know yet how to read or write. Only actors and labels have changed. The 'knowledge society' has created a new focus of richness as well as of poverty, it has made new divides and differences appear, and it has invented contemporary forms of social exclusion and illiteracy. A very important part of the world still remains under the shadow of social development and progress, whereas the most influential ones – no matter what they say – continue to control the rest, holding in their hands the enormous power of information, while multinational corporations have put a price on the most valuable knowledge (medicine, biology, engineering, agriculture, genetics, computing and telecommunication) swelling their coffers.

Only those who can afford it will be able to have access to information. Authors' rights under restrictive conditions make it very difficult to have access to literature and the arts. Nowadays, culture is a privilege of the very few who can pay for it and its free distribution has become almost illegal. Accessible knowledge on the Internet – plenty in quantity and varied in quality – can only be reached by those who have technological capacity and necessary training. Information power is still in the hands of very few, but extremely powerful people. Furthermore, the machinery of this system has created a sophisticated chain of subtle links that make it difficult to break. Poor societies are left behind and their disadvantaged people continue living in misery in our world, among us, with us, and because of us.

The librarian has seen this long process happen since the first symbols were inscribed in clay tablets or parchments. Over the centuries, the library role has adapted itself quickly to the new demands of its users: from merely storing documents to being a nest of controversial intellectuals, a refuge for works of classical literature in dark times, a showcase for priceless treasures, a basic knowledge source, a provider of both development and memory support. Many librarians have worked as accomplices to the powerful. But many others have fought for literacy teaching and knowledge diffusion, campaigned for free expression, struggled for free access to information, and promoted equality and solidarity.

The librarian has not always been conscious of all the power resting in his/her hands, nor of the huge responsibility for making fair use of it.

Immersed in the traditional activities of preservation and organisation, maybe confused with the vertiginous changes that have recently taken place, the librarian does not seem to notice the important part they might play in the present society. They should guarantee liberties and human rights such as education, information access, free expression, identity and work. They should provide practical tools so users can solve for themselves health problems, prevent violence, addictions and nutritional deficiencies. The librarian should wipe out illiteracy, revitalise oral traditions, spread ancient and almost forgotten knowledge, and recover endangered languages. They should fight against racism and discrimination, teach tolerance and respect, and facilitate integration in multicultural societies. The librarian should give voice to ever-silent peoples, encourage those who failed to reach their goal, and extend their hand towards the weakest ones. They should demonstrate age, gender, religion, and race equality among all peoples. The librarian should spread solidarity and brotherhood, tell the story of those who were defeated, express admiration for every little example of our wonderful human diversity and bring back seemingly insignificant memories that prove to be invaluable as time passes. They should promote free democratic and socially egalitarian access to information by liberating us from any restraints on its flow due to commercial chains. The librarian should pursue the laudable aim of keeping power from the hands of the minority. They should be able to achieve some sort of equilibrium by demolishing certain walls and building new bridges. The librarian should help people to look in each other's eyes on an equal footing. The librarian should do it not because it is a good idea but because this *is* the idea.

This guide clearly demonstrates that many librarians are aware of the power they have and their responsibility of using it fairly. They have already assumed an active, creative, imaginative, consistent and supportive role in their job and, consequently, in our society. Toni Samek's work also gives evidence of many librarians waking up from a hundred-year-old dream and being able to knock out their library's walls, open the bookcases, and allow books to reach every corner of their communities. Her work tells us about those librarians who dare to shout and dream at the same time that they recognise the painful reality that surrounds them. These professionals are always trying to find solutions for users' needs and interests by working next to them. They, as the author proves, have to be organised, have to investigate, propose, design, plan and discuss. Many of them demonstrate, protest, show their disagreement and turn their place of work and their life into true trenches, fighting for their ideals of peace, justice, freedom, equality and hope. This guide demonstrates that utopia is still alive. And provided that it exists, there will be always good reasons for going on and giving our best.

As a librarian and also as an anarchist, I believe and desire that the words and the information that my friend and colleague, Toni Samek, sets free and spreads in these pages will manage to blow open locked doors, melt the chains from thousands of minds, and push many to undertake the battle that does not need gunfire to be fought: the battle for freedom.

Edgardo Civallero
Córdoba (Argentina), June 2006

Prefacio

La información representa poder. Poder económico, social, político, humano... El poder para manejar recursos, para generar bienestar, para controlar vidas... Y un poder tan grande siempre está en manos de unos pocos. Muy pocas veces se comparte.

Desde el amanecer de los tiempos, la información permitió comprender los ritmos de la naturaleza y aprovechar sus recursos. Fue entonces cuando los campos dieron a luz enormes cosechas, los ríos fueron domados y canalizados, las rocas y el adobe se elevaron en murallas, pirámides y *zigurats*, las enfermedades comenzaron a ser curadas y el hierro y el vidrio comenzaron a ser modelados. Toda esa información fue cuidadosamente protegida por minorías privilegiadas: chamanes, jefes y maestros artesanos.

Con el surgimiento de las ciudades y la progresiva complejización de las estructuras sociales, surgió la escritura como una herramienta necesaria para la organización del trabajo, los excedentes y las riquezas, o quizás para la preservación de una naciente pirámide social que se perpetuaría por siglos. Los cotizados escribas administraron los recursos humanos y materiales disponibles (dirigiendo los beneficios a las arcas de los ricos), escribieron historias (según la versión de los vencedores), proclamaron la excelencia de las castas gobernantes, loaron a los héroes y los dioses oficiales y anotaron las leyes del cielo y de la tierra, es decir, las normas que debían regir en esta vida y en la del Más Allá.

La escritura conservó para la posteridad una parte -mínima- del conocimiento humano, pero al mismo tiempo creó una de las barreras más implacables que ha sufrido el hombre: el analfabetismo. Los canales orales siguieron funcionando (hasta la actualidad) pero el conocimiento y la información estratégica se encerraron para siempre en el misterio de los signos escritos. En consecuencia, conocer la escritura y controlar la información significó poder: el poder que posee el que sabe.

Hasta el nacimiento de los sistemas de impresión, la información se mantuvo codificada en las tiras de fibras de los sacerdotes mayas y aztecas, en los códices de pergamino de los monasterios europeos, en los manuscritos islámicos y judíos, en las tablillas de bambú del Asia sudoriental o en las bandas de seda chinas. El resto continuó transmitiéndose de boca en boca, de generación en generación, e incluso así, el conocimiento oral más valioso quedaba en manos de algunos elegidos.

El saber permitió la mejora de técnicas de navegación y medicina que llevaron al descubrimiento de nuevos horizontes externos e internos; permitió el desarrollo de ingenios y artefactos que mejoraron la agricultura y la industria; permitió el crecimiento y el progreso económico... Pero también permitió la creación de armas que mataran en forma más eficiente. Todo aquello que tiene un lado luminoso tiene también un lado oscuro, y el saber no iba a ser la excepción.

Con la imprenta el conocimiento se liberó, los libros llegaron a millones de manos y con ellos se difundió el placer de la lectura y las posibilidades de la escritura. Leer significó expresar y aprehender ideas nuevas, ejercer derechos y libertades, cortar cadenas, aflojar mordazas... Sin embargo, la información realmente importante continuó en manos de minorías cultas: los científicos, los filósofos, los aristócratas...

Las clepsidras de la historia derramaron sus aguas lenta e inexorablemente. El mundo presenció revoluciones sociales e industriales, guerras sin sentido, maravillosos descubrimientos, hambre y muerte, plagas y enfermedades, hongos nucleares y manifestaciones por la paz, monstruos vencidos y fantasmas por vencer... De una forma o de otra, el saber jugó un papel crucial en todos esos acontecimientos. Y, de una forma o de otra, tal saber estuvo siempre en manos de unos pocos. El progreso, el desarrollo, el 'Primer Mundo', la riqueza, el bienestar y el crecimiento sólo beneficiaron a una minoría: una enorme mayoría continuó del otro lado del gran muro de la educación, de la alfabetización, de la (in)formación, conservando a duras penas identidades y culturas e intentando sobrevivir en un mundo que los dejaba atrás, siempre atrás y abajo.

Hoy la información se ha convertido en un bien de consumo, el eje en torno al cual gira el actual paradigma socio-económico: la 'Sociedad del Conocimiento'. La (r)evolución digital y el desarrollo diario de las tecnologías de telecomunicación permiten recuperar, almacenar y manejar conocimiento, permiten estar en contacto permanente, veloz y directo con puntos lejanos del planeta y permiten llevar una biblioteca en el bolsillo, en una sencilla chapa de plástico.

Pero, a pesar de tantos descubrimientos y creaciones y de tantas nuevas puertas abiertas, el sistema y la estructura siguen igual: poco ha cambiado. Aún hay informados y desinformados, aún hay pueblos enteros condenados a la ignorancia y al silencio, aún hay analfabetos, aún hay ricos y pobres. Sólo han cambiado las etiquetas y los actores. La 'Sociedad del Conocimiento' ha generado nuevos núcleos de poder, ha creado nuevas brechas y diferencias y ha inventado nuevos analfabetismos. Una gran parte del mundo continúa a la sombra del desarrollo social y del progreso mientras los poderosos de siempre -a pesar de sus discursos- mantienen el poder en sus manos y las compañías multinacionales ponen precio al saber valioso (medicina, biología, ingeniería, agricultura, genética, informática, telecomunicaciones) y alimenta sus cuentas bancarias.

La información pasó a ser propiedad de aquel que puede pagarla. Los férreos derechos de autor hacen que incluso el arte y la literatura sean para los que puedan comprarlos y que la libre difusión se convierta en algo casi ilegal. El conocimiento disponible en las redes digitales -abundante en cantidad y diverso en calidad- solo puede ser accedido por aquellos que dispongan de la tecnología y los conocimientos adecuados.

El poder de la información sigue estando en manos de unos pocos, y los mecanismos que reproducen este sistema se han vuelto muy sutiles. Las sociedades pobres, desventajadas, dejadas atrás (porque para que exista el poder y el poderoso debe existir su contraparte) siguen aquí, junto a nosotros, entre nosotros, con nosotros. Por nosotros.

El bibliotecario ha sido testigo de todo este largo proceso desde que se escribió el primer signo sobre una tableta de arcilla o un papiro. El rol de la biblioteca ha ido cambiando a lo largo de los siglos, adaptándose flexiblemente a las necesidades de aquellos a quienes sirvió. De mero depósito de documentos pasó a ser nido de intelectuales, refugio de clásicos en edades oscuras, escaparate de tesoros adornados, fuente de saber básico, apoyo al desarrollo y gestora de memorias. Muchas veces ha sido cómplice del poderoso y lo ha servido. Muchas otras ha luchado por la alfabetización y la difusión del conocimiento, por la libre expresión y el libre acceso al saber, por la igualdad y la solidaridad.

El bibliotecario pocas veces ha sido consciente del poder que descansa en sus manos y de la inmensa responsabilidad que significa gestionarlo. Inmerso en sus actividades tradicionales de conservación y organización, mareado quizás por los cambios vertiginosos que le han traído los nuevos tiempos, el bibliotecario parece no darse cuenta del importantísimo rol que puede jugar en la sociedad actual.

Puede garantizar libertades y derechos humanos, tales como educación, información, libre expresión, identidad, trabajo... Puede proporcionar herramientas para la solución de problemas de salud, violencia, adicciones y nutrición... Puede borrar todo tipo de analfabetismo, puede recuperar tradición oral, puede difundir conocimientos perdidos y recuperar lenguas en peligro.... Puede luchar contra el racismo y la discriminación, puede enseñar la tolerancia y el respeto, puede facilitar la integración en sociedades multiculturales... Puede dar voz a los que son mantenidos en silencio, fuerzas a los caídos, manos a los débiles... Puede demostrar la igualdad de todos los seres humanos, de todos los sexos, edades, credos y razas... Puede difundir la solidaridad y la fraternidad, puede contar la historia de los vencidos, puede expresar las facetas mínimas de una maravillosa diversidad humana, puede perpetuar memorias insignificantes y grandiosas... Puede difundir el acceso abierto, puede liberar información de sus cadenas comerciales...Puede lograr que, por una vez en la historia, el poder no permanezca en las manos de unos pocos. Puede lograr cierto equilibrio. Puede derribar murallas y tender puentes. Puede hacer que los hombres logren mirarse a los ojos de igual a igual.

En realidad, no *puede* hacerlo. *Debe* hacerlo.

Esta Guía demuestra claramente que muchos bibliotecarios ya han reconocido ese poder y ese deber y han asumido un rol social activo, creativo, imaginativo, consecuente y solidario. Demuestra que muchos han despertado de un sueño de siglos, han derribado los muros de sus bibliotecas, han desencadenado los estantes y han hecho llegar libros y saber a cada rincón de sus comunidades. Demuestra que muchos bibliotecarios gritan y sueñan, reconocen la dolorosa realidad que los rodea y buscan soluciones para los problemas y las necesidades de sus usuarios trabajando a su lado... La autora muestra en este texto que muchos se organizan, investigan, proponen, construyen, dialogan... Muestra que muchos se manifiestan, protestan, se quejan y convierten sus lugares de trabajo y sus vidas en verdaderas trincheras, peleando por sus ideales: paz, justicia, libertad, igualdad, esperanza…

Esta Guía demuestra que *la utopía no ha muerto*. Y mientras exista la utopía, existirán motivos para seguir adelante. Como bibliotecario y como anarquista, confío y deseo que las palabras y la información que mi amiga y colega Toni Samek libera y difunde en estas páginas logren reventar los muros y derretir las cadenas de miles de mentes, y empujen a muchos a comprometerse en esta lucha sin armas. La lucha por la libertad.

Edgardo Civallero
Córdoba (Argentina), junio 2006

Acknowledgments

First thanks to Ruth Rikowski for inviting me to write for Chandos Publishing, to Glyn Jones for accepting this project for the Chandos catalogue, and to the sisters and brothers at Information for Social Change for believing in such work.

Warmest of thanks to the following friends and colleagues for their kind and generous support for me and for this project: Ali Abdi, Anna Altmann, Sanford Berman, Michele Besant, John Buschman, Jennifer Branch, Elizabeth Buchanan, Johannes Britz, Brian Campbell, Rafael Capurro, Toni Carbo, James Danky, Annette de Faveri, Kathleen de la Peña McCook, Shiraz Durrani, Paloma Fernández de Avilés, Dawn Ford, Thomas Froehlich, Sabina Iseli-Otto, Wallace Koehler, KR, Rory Litwin, Margaret Mackey, Elaine MacLean, Gustavo Navarro, Dai Newman, Diane Oberg, Christine Pawley, Lisa Sloniowski, Paul Sturges, Darlene Syrotuik, Louise Robbins, Tara Robertson, Loriene Roy, Mark Rozenzweig, Alvin Schrader, Ali Shiri, Lynette Shultz, SLIS students through time, Marti Smith, Sam Trosow, Lennart Wettmark, Paul Whitney, Wayne Wiegand, Christine Wiesenthal, Charles Willett and Nancy Zimmerman.

Special thanks to the exceptional and most generous contributions of Edgardo Civallero (friend and foreword contributor), Kenneth Gariepy (friend, contributing editor and indexer), Anna-Marie Klassen (friend and research assistant). Raw and heartfelt thanks to family for sharing their wonder and wisdom at all ages: Robert Samek (in memory), Krystyna Samek, Tarun Ghose, Rob Samek, Jan Harkness Samek, Diane Misick and John Misick. Last but not least, eternal thanks to my husband and to our children, for making this book a family affair of living and learning from the breakfast table to lights out: Burton Howell, Nikki Howell and Rudy Howell.

The School of Library and Information Studies, Faculty of Education, University of Alberta provided generous support for this project through its sponsorship of graduate student assistance.

This project received $2,000 in critical financial support from the Advancement of Scholarship Fund awarded by the Faculty of Education, University of Alberta.

Fifty per cent of any personal profit that may (or may not) be made from this book will be given to the 'Fundacion Mempo Giardinelli' (*http://www.fundamgiardinelli.org.ar/fundacion.htm*). Mempo Giardinelli is a writer, who uses his funds for work on education and literacy. The Tempo Giardinelli Foundation is a non-profit non-governmental organisation 'whose essential mission is to promote and foster reading. It is an educational institution that carries out activities and programs through a study centre while trying to fulfill the present and future culture demand in Chaco and all the Northeast region of Argentina. In addition, it is a common cause institution which supports reading-related social programs.'

Preface

In 1983, at its 49th General Conference in Munich, the International Federation of Library Associations and Institutions (IFLA) adopted the Resolution on Behalf of Librarians Who Are Victims of Violation of Human Rights. The resolution recognises the risks that library workers take to uphold core library values such as intellectual freedom. It states:

> In the name of human rights, librarians must, as a profession, express their solidarity with those of their colleagues who are persecuted for their opinions, wherever they may be. The Council mandates the President of IFLA, when informed of specific cases, after due considerations to intervene when appropriate with competent authorities on behalf of these colleagues.

In 1989, IFLA achieved global coverage when it expanded the text of the Munich Resolution and adopted its Resolution on Freedom of Expression, Censorship and Libraries. This resolution

> encourages librarians and their associations globally to support the enforcement of Article 19 of the Universal Declaration of Human Rights, to exchange information on the abuse of restrictions of freedom of expression which concern them and, when necessary, to refer the matter to the President of IFLA and if applicable to other competent international organizations, non-governmental or intergovernmental.[1]

(Article 19 directs, 'Everyone has the right to freedom of opinion and expression; this right includes freedom to hold opinions without interference and to seek, receive and impart information and ideas through any media and regardless of frontiers.')[2] The resolution also instructs the President of IFLA 'to intervene in the most appropriate way with relevant authorities about freedom of expression and to cooperate, if necessary and to this end, with other international organizations.'[3] For example, an IFLA press release, dated 18 November 2005, states:

> Participating in the World Summit on the Information Society (WSIS) in Tunisia, IFLA most strongly protests the abuses on intellectual freedom in the country. With deep concern we have witnessed the attempts by Tunisian authorities to silence journalists and human rights activists in the run up and during the summit. Human rights activists have been imprisoned and some are on hunger strike. Journalists have been attacked, civil society meetings cancelled as a protest to the state of affairs. Information has been censored, newspapers banned and websites blocked. IFLA supports the Tunisian Monitoring Group's (TMG) appeal to UN Secretary General Mr Kofi Annan 'to call on the Tunisian authorities to end attacks on civil society and freedom of expression not only during this Summit, but beyond and to initiate an Office of the High Commissioner on Human Rights special investigation into the occurrences around the WSIS.'[4]

Despite the good intentions of Article 19, and the 1989 resolution supporting Article 19, existing social, economic, cultural, political and ideological pressures that affect library and information work have led to the not uncommon practice of internal or self-censorship by library and information workers. Few regions (Latin America, Portugal, Sri Lanka, UK) have sanctions in place in the event that librarians violate their code of professional ethics, which in many instances worldwide instruct library and information workers to uphold intellectual freedom and to combat censorship.[5] Although intellectual freedom is the first contemporary core value embraced by IFLA, the vast majority of library and information workers worldwide do not benefit from any protection afforded by freedom of workplace speech on 'non-confidential professional and policy matters about the operation of the library and matters of public concern within the framework of applicable laws.'[6] A disturbing situation has evolved in which library and information workers advocate on behalf of their users for those very rights and freedoms they themselves have been denied. This book documents social action strategies used by library and information workers worldwide to negotiate this fundamental barrier in support of human rights in the face of adversity and risk. These strategies represent library and information workers' political and transformative acts of resistance to ideological domination in the present reality of war, revolution, social change and global market fundamentalism. Some of the strategies documented in this book involve varying degrees of personal and professional risk depending on the political, legal, economic, ideological, technological and cultural contexts of the countries and communities in which library and information workers live and labour, as well as more personal factors such as the gender, class, sexual orientation, citizenship, disability, ethnic origin, geographical location, language, political philosophy, race or religion of library and information workers themselves. It is time we fully recognised the political context of library and information work. As Shiraz Durrani observes:

> manipulation of information, whether conscious or unconscious, is an important matter, not only in local life, but in international relations as well. Librarians can become tools in the hands of those seeking to manipulate whole populations to think along their lines – or stand firm to support the democratic rights of the people manipulated. There is no third way here.[7]

To avoid becoming a tool in the hands of those who seek to manipulate others, and in order to support core library values, as well as giving due attention to global democratic and human rights, the priority for twenty-first century librarianship is to act on IFLA's 1983 and 1989 human rights resolutions. Failing to do so could result in Heinrich Heine's dire warning, that 'where they have burned books, they will end in burning human beings',[8] becoming more of a reality than it already is. Many of the strategies showcased in this book are practised in the international critical library community, where considerations for the human condition and for human rights take precedence over other professional concerns. This critical community, from which this book draws upon for its optimistic vision for the future, has built up its visibility and momentum over the course of many decades. For historical context, the chronological formation of select critical library groups is outlined below:

- 1939–1944: Progressive Librarians' Guild (PLG) – USA;
- 1969: Social Responsibilities Round Table (SRRT) of the American Library Association (ALA) – USA;
- 1969: Bibliotek i Samhälle (BIS) – Sweden;
- 1983: Arbeitskreis kritischer Bibliothekarinnen und Bibliothekare (KRIBIBI) – Austria;

- 1988: Arbeitskreis kritischer BibliothekarInnen (AKRIBIE) – Germany;
- 1990: Progressive Librarians Guild (PLG) – USA;
- 1990: Library and Information Workers Organization (LIWO) – South Africa;
- 1994: Information for Social Change (ISC) – UK
- 1997: Social Responsibilities Discussion Group of the International Federation of Library Associations and Institutions (IFLA) – La Hague;
- 2000: Círculode Estudios sobre Bibliotecología Política y Social (CEBI) – Study Circle on Political and Social Librarianship – Mexico;
- 2001: Progressive Librarians' International Coalition (PLIC) – Sweden;
- 2003: Grupo de Estudios Sociales en Bibliotecología y Document-atcíon (GESBI) – Social Studies Group on Librarianship and Documentation – Argentina;
- 2005: Progressive African Library & Information Activists' Group (PALIAct) – Africa.

Disclaimer

This book is intended as an accessible and practical starting point to lay the foundation in support of ethical thinking on the moral responsibilities of library and information workers. Although it has many elements that draw on scholarship, *Librarianship and Human Rights: A Twenty-First Century Guide* is not meant to be a scholarly book. It forgoes the formal apparatus that a scholarly work would require, though direct quotations are well referenced and sources are included.[9]

This book makes connections between twenty-first century library and information work worldwide *and* aspects of the Universal Declaration of Human Rights (1948).

This book does not suggest that articles expressed in, or proposed for inclusion in, the Universal Declaration of Human Rights (1948) are universal or absolute, or even appropriate for all peoples.[10]

This book acknowledges issues of higher magnitude than human rights, such as sustainable development and peace not war.[11]

The intellectual content of this book is informed by library and information work worldwide, however, heavy concentration is limited to English language sources and sources translated into English.

A three-step agenda for this book

First, this book encourages library and information workers to take a stand in the ongoing debate about what constitutes library work.

Second, this book uses library and information rhetoric related to human rights (e.g. freedom of expression, freedom of thought, freedom of inquiry, privacy, confidentiality) as an entrée to taking a professional interest in broad issues such as sustainable development, pandemics, poverty, war and peace, torture, destruction of cultural resources and government intimidation.

Third, this book conceives the library as a point of resistance. [12]

Aims of this book

This book aims to raise awareness about existing and proposed elements of the Universal Declaration of Human Rights (1948) that relate particularly to core library values, information ethics and global information justice.

This book aims to encourage library and information workers and other stakeholders in information and knowledge societies to participate locally, nationally and internationally in dialogue, collaboration, organisation, empathy, decision-making, practice, philosophy and policy development to promote the amelioration of social problems.

This book aims to identify examples of diversity and contestation within library and information work, especially related to the subject of intellectual freedom.

This book aims to disseminate broad aims of critical librarianship.

This book aims to expand the traditional library conception of intellectual freedom.

This book aims to counter library neutrality with respect to cultural, political and economic matters.

This book aims to contribute to the development of a full institutional memory of librarianship; one that provides identity to a diversity of library and information voices.

Features of this book

- This book is the first monograph of its kind.
- This book places librarianship front and centre in knowledge societies.
- This book threads library core values through information ethics and the global information justice movement.
- This book documents a range of critical library and information work worldwide.
- This book portrays library and information workers as participants and interventionists in social conflicts.
- This book has urgent purpose.
- This book is committed to an optimistic vision.
- This books fits in line with other early twenty-first century works that explore civic engagement in cultural networks.

Notes

1. IFLA (1989) Resolution on Freedom of Expression, Censorship and Libraries, adopted by the 55th IFLA Council and General Conference, Paris, 1989. Available at: *http://www.ifla.org/faife/policy/paris_e.htm* (accessed 26 October 2006).
2. Universal Declaration of Human Rights. Available at: *http://www.un.org/Overview/rights.html* (accessed 26 October 2006).
3. IFLA (1989), op. cit.
4. IFLA/FAIFE (2005) 'IFLA protests crack down of intellectual freedom in Tunisia', press release, 18 November. Available at: *http://www.ifla.org/V/press/Pr-18112005.htm* (accessed 26 October 2006).
5. Shachaf, P. (2005) 'A global perspective on library association codes of ethics', presented at the Association for Library and Information Science Education Annual Conference: Boundary Crossings, 13 January, Boston, MA. Available at: *http://ella.slis.indiana.edu/~shachaf/ALISE%202005.ppt* (accessed 26 October 2006).
6. American Library Association (2005) Resolution on Workplace Speech. Adopted 26 June 2005.
7. Culture, Media and Sport Committee (2005) 'Public libraries: Third Report of Session 2004–05'. Available at: *http://www.publications.parliament.uk/pa/cm200405/cmselect/cmcumeds/81/81i.pdf* (accessed 26 October 2006).
8. 'Dort, wo man Bücher verbrennt, verbrennt man am Ende auch Menschen.'

From Heinrich Heine's play *Almansor* (1821). See *http://www.ala.org/ ala/oif/bannedbooksweek/bookburning/bookburning.htm* (accessed 26 October 2006).

9. This disclaimer point borrows from language used by Lerner, F. (1998) *The Story of Libraries: From the Invention of Writing to the Computer Age*, New York: The Continuum International Publishing Group Inc.; i.

10. Thanks to Brian Campbell for encouraging me to read and think critically about human rights discourse.

11. Thanks to Alvin Schrader for his clarity on this point.

12. Special thanks to Mark Rosenzweig for first introducing me to the concept of the library as a point of resistance.

About the author

Toni Samek is as an educator and scholar at the School of Library and Information Studies, University of Alberta, Edmonton, Alberta, Canada.

Toni's education includes a Doctor of Philosophy (Library and Information Studies) from the University of Wisconsin-Madison (USA), a Master of Library and Information Studies from Dalhousie University (Halifax, Nova Scotia, Canada), and an Honours Bachelor of Arts from the University of Toronto (Ontario, Canada).

Toni's teaching, research and service interests include critical librarianship, intercultural information ethics, global information justice, human rights, intellectual and academic freedom, social responsibility, library history and library education.

Toni holds the following positions in the library and information community:

- Advisory Board Member, 2005–, Information for Social Change;
- Information Ethics Fellow, 2006–07, Center for Information Policy Research, School of Information Studies, University of Wisconsin-Milwaukee, USA;
- Convenor, 2005–, Advisory Committee on Intellectual Freedom, Canadian Library Association; and
- Convenor, 2005–2007, Information Ethics Special Interest Group, Association for Library and Information Science Education.

Toni is the author of the 2001 book *Intellectual Freedom and Social Responsibility in American Librarianship, 1967–1974*, published by McFarland & Company Inc, Publishers. The Kyoto University Library and Information Science Study Group published the Japanese translation in 2003. The historical work examines the American Library Association's profound and contentious professional identity crisis during the Vietnam conflict. The book's present-day relevance is most notable in its treatment of library neutrality and librarianship in time of war, revolution and social change ... just where *Librarianship and Human Rights: A twenty-first century guide* picks up!

The author may be contacted as follows:

Toni Samek
Associate Professor & Graduate Coordinator
School of Library & Information Studies
3-15 Rutherford South
University of Alberta
Edmonton
Alberta T6G 2J4
Canada

Tel: +1 (780) 492 0179
Fax: +1 (780) 492 2430
E-mail: *toni.samek@ualberta.ca*
Web: *http://www.ualberta.ca/~asamek/toni.htm*

Part One: The Rhetoric

'There is more to life than increasing its speed.'
Mohandas Gandhi

An urgent context for twenty-first century librarianship

This chapter explores the role of the librarian and the library in society and prepares the reader for making connections between library and information work and pressing social issues. This exploration takes a global perspective, using the rhetoric of IFLA (1927)[1] as a conceptual foundation for librarianship and human rights.

> In 1993, 'Bosnia's national and University Library, a handsome Moorish-revival building built in the 1890s on the Sarajevo riverfront, was shelled and burned … Bombarded with incendiary grenades from Serbian nationalist positions across the river, the library burned for three days; most of its irreplaceable contents were reduced to ashes. Braving a line of sniper fire, librarians and citizen volunteers formed a human chain to pass books out of the burning building. Interviewed by an ABC News camera[man], one of them said: 'We managed to save just a few very precious books. Everything else burned down. And a lot of our heritage, national heritage, lay down in the ashes'. Among the human casualties was Aida Buturovi librarian in the National Library's international exchanges section, shot to death by a sniper.[2]

András Riedlmayer continues:

> throughout Bosnia, libraries, archives and cultural institutions have been targeted for destruction in an attempt to eliminate the material evidence, books, documents and works of art that could remind future generations that people of different ethnic and religious traditions once shared a common heritage in Bosnia. In

the towns and villages of occupied Bosnia, communal records (cathedral registers, endowment documents, parish records) of more than 800 Muslim and Bosnian Croat (Catholic) communities have been torched by Serb nationalist forces as part of 'ethnic cleansing' campaigns. While the destruction of a community's institutions and records is, in fact the first instance, part of a strategy of intimidation aimed at driving out members of the targeted groups, it also serves a long-term goal. These records were proof that non-Serbs once resided and owned property in that place, that they had historical roots there. By burning the documents, by razing mosques and Catholic churches and bulldozing the graveyards, the nationalist forces who have now taken over these towns and villages are trying to insure themselves against any future claims by which people they have driven out and dispossessed. Other Bosnians, however, remain determined to preserve their country's historic ideal of a multicultural, tolerant society and the institutions that enshrine collective memory.[3]

Library and information workers play an important role in preserving and supporting the ideals of tolerance, democracy, human rights and collective memory in many volatile parts of the world.

As Argentine Nobel Peace Prize winner Adolfo Pérez Esquivel observes:

freedom of the press is being threatened, as is the heritage of the peoples and their cultures which are being subdued by the prevailing globalization. Social and cultural resistance is fundamental for the sake of freedom and the rights of individuals and peoples ... you, who are the ones in charge of preserving memory ... can contribute ... [and resist] an 'only way of thinking' ... that leads to the destruction of identity and culture.[4]

Wayne Wiegand, however, warns that librarianship is 'a profession much more interested in process and structure than in people'.[5] Jack Andersen, meanwhile, cautions that library and information studies have

managed to create a metaphysical discourse that tends to favor technical and managerial language use. Such language does not invite critical consciousness and analysis as it is distanced from the objects it is talking about. Indeed, technical and managerial language often stands in opposition to basic human needs, and is more concerned with how to do things rather than describe and critically discuss how these things (i.e. knowledge organization systems) work or do not.[6]

Edgardo Civallero urges the field of library and information studies

> to give up its silence, its marble tower, its privileged positions in the new knowledge society, its apolitical attitudes and its objectivity. It must become more deeply involved in the problems, side with the helpless and struggle, shoulder to shoulder (maybe without tools, without technology, without money, just equipped with imagination, working wishes and service vocation) with other human beings, who were – and currently are – forgotten, just because they are faithful to themselves.[7]

A concrete example of the trend towards process rather than people can be seen in the rise in contemporary North American public libraries of 'customer behaviour expectations' developed for and targeted at 'poor, especially homeless, persons'.

American library activist Sanford Berman brings our attention to a city-county library in San Luis Obispo County, California that developed a policy to ban 'offensive body odor' and 'sleeping in the library', as well as to Houston, Texas where the City Council passed a series of new library regulations that prohibit 'using rest rooms for bathing' and ban 'large amounts of personal possessions'.[8] Berman *outs* these policies, [coupled with the increase in use of security staff] in the public library, as contributions to the erosion of public space and criminalisation of the poor. These policies do nothing to ameliorate the root problem of poverty. As Berman bluntly states: 'the *problem* is not *smelly, unkempt patrons*, but rather poverty itself and our unwillingness to combat it'.[9] Meanwhile, despite the American Library Association's own Policy 61 (Library Services to Poor People),

> barriers to library use by low-income people abound and the profession itself has largely ignored Policy 61's strictures to involve poor people and anti-poverty advocates in local decision-making, lobby for poverty-reducing legislation (like living wage laws, affordable housing, national health insurance, and adequate welfare payments), promote greater public awareness of poverty-related issues and relevant library resources, and eliminate economic obstacles like fines and fees.[10]

Wiegand's, Andersen's, and Civallero's warnings and Berman's exposé echo information ethicist Rafael Capurro's 1992 warning that:

> an information economy that seeks to reduce 'information' to an exchange value without taking into account the different 'forms of life' in which it is grounded is no less dangerous than a blind exploitation of nature. In designing tools, we are designing ... ways of being ... Information science ... must accomplish a self-reflection in a formal-interpretive as well as in a cultural-historical way. It has to resist the temptation to become a purely technical heuristics or a meta-discipline embracing ethics and politics.[11]

Indeed, as expressed by the fledgling Canadian Libraries in Communities interest group, there is an urgent need to 'challenge the broader library community to reflect on how our fundamental values of inclusiveness have drifted in the pursuit of efficiency and quantification ... [and to recognise that] there is more to library engagement than checklists and programs'.[12]

In a similar vein, Herbert I. Schiller suggests that the focus on technology in the library and information curriculum

> serves to delude many, librarians included, that the new means to achieve status and respect is to concentrate on the *machinery* of information, production and transmission. When and if this focus turns rigidly exclusive, wittingly or not, the *social* basis of the profession and the needs of the majority of the people are left unattended.[13]

Schiller finds 'no inherent incompatibility in offering more technologically-oriented courses in a library school and maintaining, indeed, expanding the school's attention to social issues of the new instrumentation'. This, he argues, 'should be the aim of a new librarianship curriculum – how to guarantee social use and application of the new information technologies. But this is not what is happening. Instead, there are different vistas.'[14]

Christine Pawley concurs with these critical voices, and advocates that we carry our collective conscience into library and information studies education, because she finds that education 'perpetuates rather than transforms the status quo'.[15] In particular, Pawley observes 'four focal areas that relate to the theory and practice of cultural hegemony [that] have preoccupied the LIS curricular fields: links with corporate world, professionalization, aspiration to scientific status, and stratification of literacy and of institutions'.[16] 'From a class perspective', she asserts, the 'failure of LIS education to confront societal questions is itself a sign of the power of the dominant class to exercise hegemony'.[17] Pawley indicates we would better serve students by preparing them to 'tackle broader political questions relating to control of the production, distribution, and indeed, definition of information'.[18] A key challenge then for twenty-first century library and information communities, starting with educators such as this author, is to foster language and a culture of critical librarianship which better support core library values and that encourage and promote active participation in the amelioration of social problems. This challenge is considerable, but we have begun the hard work.

In this book, the reader will encounter urgent library and information voices reflecting contemporary local, national and transnational calls to action on conflicts generated by failures to acknowledge human rights, by struggles for recognition and representation, by social exclusion and by the library institution's role in these conflicts. These powerful voices have integrated library and information work into existing social movements as well as the global discourse on human rights. These voices not only depict library and information workers as political actors, but challenge existing networks of control by providing new possibilities for strategies of resistance.

This book's approach to library and information work is grounded in practical, critical and emancipatory terms; social action is a central theme. Social action in the context of library and information work involves actions on and reactions to events that occur in the library's broader social context (e.g. new anti-terrorism legislation). Historically, the profession's claim to library neutrality has drawn a line between professional issues such as literacy and so-called non-library issues such as war. A similar line has categorically divided library advocacy and library activism. This book strongly supports the international library movement known in the twenty-first century as *critical librarianship*, which aims to blur these lines and to expose them as both counter-intuitive and counter-productive to the development of more humanistic (and less techno-managerial) library and information work. This book is conceived as a direct challenge to the notion of library neutrality, especially in the present context of war, revolution, social change and global market fundamentalism. This book views library and information workers as active participants and interventionists in social conflicts. Ideally, this book will help to break down the constraints imposed by the myth of library neutrality that divorces library and information work from participation in social struggle, and makes the profession vulnerable to control networks such as economic or political regimes.[19]

'Taking sides on whether or not the profession is neutral is a debate about the nature and ideology of librarianship.'[20] Despite the dominant view that librarianship is a neutral profession, Colin Darch observes, 'librarians have always been politically engaged, despite themselves'.[21] For example, the 2005 library seminar 'Libraries in Times of War, Revolution & Social Change' examined

> books and libraries as agents of cultural memory to be protected, appropriated or obliterated; library collections and services as instruments of political power in providing, restricting or withholding access to information; libraries as places of refuge, solace and practical help in times of social disruption; libraries and their contents as cultural heritage and as booty; the nature of the revolutionary cultural and political regimes in which libraries are situated with regard to literacy and learning; [and] the responsibilities of the international community in creating and enforcing policies and procedures of protection, reconstitution and restitution of cultural artifacts, including books and libraries.[22]

Examining relationships in society among people, information, recorded knowledge and the cultural record exposes local, national and international issues[23] related to the 'production, collection, interpretation, organization, preservation, storage, retrieval, dissemination, transformation and use of information' and ideas.[24] Contemporary examples include biometrics, intellectual property, global tightening of information and border controls, and public access to government information. These points are coming into sharp focus, as human rights violations have received increased attention in the twenty-first century, particularly following the events of September 11, 2001, which 'triggered the adoption of legislation, policies, and practices in the United States and around the world'.[25] Such legislation, policies and practices have considerable ethical implications for library and information work in such areas as 'access to information, privacy, civil liberties, and intellectual freedom'.[26] Rhetoric and policy development on librarianship and human rights is of significance to library and information workers in their opposition to threats to intellectual freedom and their commitment to the protection of civil liberties and civic identities. Rhetoric and policy development allow library and information workers to: (1) take a stand in the enduring dilemma about what constitutes library work; (2) use the concept of intellectual freedom as a viable means to take a professional interest in social and political issues such as war and peace, torture, destruction of cultural resources, and government intimidation, and (3) conceive the library as a point of 'resistance'.[27]

The professional interest in ethics is on the rise, and while numerous professional codes of ethics/conduct 'for librarians and other library employees adopted by national library or librarians' associations or implemented by government agencies' include the directive to uphold intellectual freedom, most librarians around the world (as noted in the preface to this book) engage in work that carries no sanctions. As Shirley Wiegand's analysis of the US Library Bill of Rights bluntly concludes: 'the ALA has no authority over library administrations'.[28] Thus, the action, coalition and alliance of library and information workers on ethical issues take on special importance. As Martha Smith observes, although the United Nations Educational, Scientific and Cultural Organization (UNESCO) 'seeks to influence members states, it does not exert governing or enforcement authority. Therefore persuasion and consensus building are its primary tools'.[29] Like UNESCO, IFLA is a leader, not an enforcer.[30] Accordingly, IFLA's 2004 President Kay Raseroka's opening address states:

> [the] first experiences of IFLA in worldwide advocacy, within the framework of the World Summit of the Information Society, have demonstrated the need and power of cooperation; with other international organizations, and among ourselves as national member associations. These are only the first steps in influencing governments to establish and maintain democratic information services, and to live up to the Universal Declaration of Human Rights [in an era of globalisation].[31]

Working down from IFLA to the local and individual level, many library and information workers participate in persuasion and consensus building, routinely contributing to the library movement through their daily defence of intellectual freedom. This activity is often practised against prevailing economic, social and political attitudes and values (e.g. global capitalism, family or community values, anti-terrorism legislation). This is increasingly the case in the context of globalisation. UNESCO outlines globalisation as:

not just about increasing the worldwide circulation of information and ideas. Economically speaking, it entails an increase in capital flow, transnational investment and international trade, thereby integrating all countries into a single giant world market. In terms of politics, the social, economic or environmental orientation of states is being increasingly determined by regional and international structures.[32]

Library rhetoric on intellectual freedom tends 'to emphasize the Western tradition, with a focus on the individual rights rather than the community cohesion'.[33] In the context of globalisation, core library values such as intellectual freedom need to be continuously revisited by individuals, institutions, and societies as a whole.

Core values ideologically 'define, inform, and guide' library and information practice. They 'reflect the history and ongoing development of the profession'. IFLA's core values are currently defined as:

> (1) the endorsement of the principles of freedom of access to information, ideas and works of imagination and freedom of expression embodied in Article 19 of the Universal Declaration of Human Rights; (2) the belief that people, communities and organizations need universal and equitable access to information, ideas and works of imagination for their social, educational, cultural, democratic and economic well-being; (3) the conviction that delivery of high quality library and information services helps guarantee that access; and, (4) the commitment to enable all Members of the Federation to engage in, and benefit from, its activities without regard to citizenship, disability, ethnic origin, gender, geographical location, language, political philosophy, race or religion.[34]

These core library values are determined by overlapping consensus. How individual library and information workers, library groups and institutions handle these values proves to be diverse.

IFLA makes an explicit connection between the library core value of intellectual freedom and human rights. This is underscored in its Statement on Libraries and Intellectual Freedom, which references Article 19 of the United Nations Declaration of Human Rights (1948).[35] Through its Free Access to Information and Freedom of Expression Committee (FAIFE), IFLA 'monitors the state of intellectual freedom within the library community worldwide, supports IFLA policy development, cooperates with other international human rights organisations, and responds to violations of free access to information and freedom of expression'. In recent years, there has been a heavy emphasis on technology and information societies. Shiraz Durrani notes that 'the rules developed at the World Trade Organisation, especially in the context of TRIPS (trade-related aspects of intellectual property rights)' prompted IFLA to express concerns over threats to 'not for profit libraries', intellectual property, and cultural diversity.[36]

Two key FAIFE policy statements (Glasgow Declaration on Libraries, Information Services and Intellectual Freedom and Internet Manifesto) are referred to in IFLA's WSIS contributions underlining the federation's commitment to intellectual freedom.[37] These efforts reinforce foundational human rights documents such as the IFLA/UNESCO Public Library Manifesto[38] (available from IFLA in 25 different languages), the IFLA School Library Manifesto (available from IFLA in 33 different languages) and UNESCO's Statement on Human Rights Research. The IFLA/UNESCO Public Library Manifesto was created in 1994 to urge communities and their libraries around the world to implement principles of intellectual freedom such as freedom of expression. The IFLA School Library Manifesto links school libraries to the broader library and information system in accord with the principles in the UNESCO Public Library Manifesto. UNESCO's Statement on Human Rights Research emphasises 'the promotion and protection of economic, social and cultural rights, especially the right to education, the right to take part in cultural life and the right to enjoy the benefits of scientific progress and its applications'.[39]

IFLA is the world body best recognised for developing rhetoric and awareness that consolidates the connection between library and information work and human rights. IFLA is also an important vehicle for helping library and information workers broaden their conception of intellectual freedom in the context of globalisation. For example, in August 2005, IFLA/FAIFE launched its world report on intellectual freedom and libraries, 'Libraries, National Security, Freedom of Information Laws and Social Responsibilities'. The report helps IFLA measure its

> progress in tackling barriers to accessing information and identifies the outstanding issues that must be confronted if libraries are to play a full part in the information society ... This [2005] edition includes 84 country reports submitted by IFLA members ... The

main findings are that the state of intellectual freedom in many parts of the world remains fragile.[40]

In particular, the report indicates:

- While Internet access across the international library community is slowly increasing, many parts of the world (e.g. Africa and Asia) still struggle against the digital divide.
- Use of Internet filtering software in libraries is increasing. This rise in use is fuelled by the problems of providing Internet access with child protection. Furthermore, acceptance of the use of filtering software is growing in many library associations.
- Librarians in many countries share concerns about the impending effects of anti-terror legislation.
- Violations of intellectual freedom affecting library users persist around the world. Censorship, restrictions of press freedom, and governmental restriction and surveillance of Internet use were reported in numerous countries (e.g. China, Egypt, Italy, Nepal and Uzbekistan).
- Library and information workers are making efforts to raise awareness of HIV and AIDS and women's access to information in many world regions; in other parts of the world, this type of library service has yet to be initiated.

These findings pose the question as to how to best proceed forward into twenty-first century library and information work.

IFLA identifies its professional priorities as supporting the role of libraries in society; defending the principle of freedom of information; promoting literacy, reading and lifelong learning; providing unrestricted access to information; balancing the intellectual property rights of authors with the needs of users; promoting resource sharing; preserving our intellectual heritage; developing library professionals; promoting standards, guidelines and best practices; supporting the infrastructure of library associations; and representing libraries in the technological marketplace. IFLA's strategic planning focuses attention on the role that information and information services play in 'world problems such as sustainable development and HIV/AIDS', as well as issues of 'indigenous knowledge systems and oral cultures' and the problematic application of intellectual property rights in these contexts.[41] In spite of the groundbreaking work done by IFLA, Shiraz Durrani cautions that:

while IFLA has done and can do a lot of good work, it remains a representative body of official Library Associations around the world, and most of them are conservative, establishment-oriented bodies. One cannot expect IFLA to be a radical organisation for change in the interest of working people around the world. But it is not necessary to have one or the other (IFLA or alternative, progressive organisations). There is room for both types of organisations. They may work together sometimes and have contradictions at other times; this is a healthy state of affairs.[42]

At the same time, Durrani argues there is an urgent need for alternative progressive organisations if libraries are to become 'more relevant to the majority of people'. Indeed, around the world, critical librarians engage in persuasion and consensus building through a diverse array of measures such as petitions, manifestos, resolutions, rallies, boycotts, alternative conference programmes, publishing, lobbying and daily information exchange to address historical inequities.

A key twenty-first century initiative now available in translation around the world is the 2004 Declaration from Buenos Aires on Information, Documentation and Libraries. This manifesto, developed by the Grupo de Estudios Sociales en Bibliotecología y Documentatcíon (Social Studies Group on Librarianship and Documentation) in Argentina and the Círculode Estudios sobre Bibliotecología Política y Social (Study Circle on Political and Social Librarianship) in Mexico recognises that:

> information, knowledge, documentation, archives, and libraries are communal cultural goods and resources based upon and promoted by democratic values, such as: freedom, equality, and social justice, as well as tolerance, respect, equity, solidarity, communities, society, and the dignity of individuals.[43]

Yet historically, marginalised populations, such as indigenous peoples, women, oral communities, and political radicals (i.e. 'the least socially and politically favored'[44]) have not been represented by the world's cultural and civic identities. In this critical view, cultural workers, such as educators, publishers, librarians, archivists and documentalists have both consciously and unconsciously participated in tasks that have resulted in concessions, absences, omissions, biases, negations (e.g. misrepresentation of racialised and immigrant cultures), broken cultural protocols, and disconnects 'between the way peoples are presented in mainstream' culture, 'including library materials' and the way people 'present themselves and their own culture'.[45] Cultural and literary canons, Library of Congress subject headings, library collections organised by Dewey Decimal and Universal Decimal classification, global information policies informed by the discourses of capital, community value/family value-based school curricula, and propagandistic textbooks of political regimes have all contributed to the problem. It is also important to consider the 'complicated and sometimes conflicting relationships among nation, regime, recorded expression, and national bibliography ... Legal deposit, in particular, is shadowed by historical overtones of state censorship and control'.[46]

In February 2005, the Progressive African Library & Information Activists' Group (PALIAct) published *The PALIAct Stand*, which 'recognises the right to relevant information as a basic human right,' yet reports how many people's 'experiences, their cultures, their very language' remain 'outside the walls of impressive library buildings'.[47] These emphatic words evoke the following questions as a subtext for this book: What are the implications for human rights of forgotten, buried and contaminated memories of individuals, societies and institutions; of a flattened cultural record? How can opportunities provided by information and communications technologies, interconnectivity and the global digital network be applied to ameliorate discriminatory knowledge practices to make them accessible to all? To what extent can improved library and information practices redress the failed promotion of cultural distinctiveness, cultural literacy, cultural democracy and democratic education? How can people working in the information and communication technologies fields (and sharing the principle that knowledge and information access is free, open and egalitarian for everybody[48]) consciously improve knowledge practices to facilitate the democratisation of information and knowledge and the prerequisite promotion of cultural diversity (including literacy in all its forms)?

Cultural diversity is a fundamental common ground for twenty-first century library and information work. UNESCO defines culture as a 'set of distinctive spiritual, material, intellectual and emotional features of society or a social group. It encompasses, in addition to art and literature, lifestyles, ways of living together, values systems, traditions and beliefs.' UNESCO advocates that 'respecting and safeguarding culture is a matter of Human Rights'. Threats to cultural diversity are reflected in the UNESCO Universal Declaration on Cultural Diversity, 'adopted unanimously by the 185 member states represented at the 31st General Conference in the wake of 9/11 on 2 November 2001. The

Declaration was born of the wish of the member states to define a standard-setting instrument, in the context of globalization, for the elaboration of their national cultural policies, while respecting international rules and fundamental rights. It is the first time the international community has possessed a legal instrument that raises cultural diversity to the rank of "common heritage of humanity". The Declaration sets out to respond to two major concerns: firstly, to ensure respect for cultural identities with the participation of all peoples in a democratic framework and, secondly, to contribute to the emergence of a favourable climate for the creativity of all, thereby making culture a factor of development.'[49] The UNESCO Universal Declaration on Cultural Diversity 'is the founding act of a new ethic being promoted by UNESCO at the dawn of the 21st century. For the first time the international community is provided with a wide-ranging standard-setting instrument to underpin its conviction that respect for cultural diversity and intercultural dialogue is one of the surest guarantees of development and peace.' [50]

Cultural diversity 'presupposes respect of fundamental freedoms, namely freedom of thought, conscience and religion, freedom of opinion and expression, and freedom to participate in the cultural life of one's choice'.[51] These same freedoms are embedded in contemporary core library values. While cultural diversity, then, is inextricably linked to core library values, library and information workers should recognise the threats to 'culture in general, and cultural diversity in particular'.[52] In 1990, Rafael Capurro identified such threats as technological colonisation of the life-world, cultural alienation, and oligarchic control of information resources.[53] More recently, according to UNESCO:

(1) Globalization, in its powerful extension of market principles, by highlighting the culture of economically powerful nations, has created new forms of inequality, thereby fostering cultural conflict rather than cultural pluralism. (2) States are increasingly unable to handle on their own the cross-border flow of ideas, images and resources that affect cultural development. (3) The growing divide in literacy (digital and conventional) has made the cultural debates and resources an increasingly élitist monopoly, divorced from the capabilities and interests of more than half the world's population who are now in danger of cultural and economical exclusion.[54]

Given these mounting negative pressures, library and information workers must routinely revisit their core values for motivation to foster language, culture and practices that promote positives such as cultural pluralism, unfettered transborder data flow, quality education for all, community access to information and communication technology, cross-border scientific knowledge-sharing, access to information, freedom of expression and Internet neutrality.[55]

There are currently some 6,000 languages existing in the world. However, they do not have the same number of speakers:

> only 4% of the languages are used by 96% of the world population; 50% of the world languages are in danger of extinction; 90% of the world's languages are not represented on the Internet; some five countries monopolize the world cultural industries trade. In the field of cinema, for instance, 88 countries out of 185 in the world have never had their own film production.[56]

When in October 2005, UNESCO adopted the new Universal Convention on Cultural Diversity at the UNESCO headquarters in Paris, it came as good news for library and information workers, who promote cultural diversity and related aspects of human rights such as the free flow of information as well as freedom of opinion and expression. But, of course, rhetoric does not always match reality, and 'free and equal access to information is a myth throughout the world, although different situations pertain in different countries. Control is more explicit and cruder in some places, more "sophisticated" and more invisible elsewhere (for example in Britain)'.[57] Twenty-first century librarianship that focuses on values such as human dignity, freedom of expression, social responsibility and cultural diversity is vulnerable to the push and pull of competing ideological, economic, technological, legal, political, cultural and social agendas. Challenges encompass such areas as intellectual property, preservation, cultural destruction, censorship, imposed technologies, public access to government information, privatisation, academic freedom, workplace speech, international relations, anonymity, privacy and confidentiality, human security, national security policies, transborder data flow and information poverty.

Furthermore, relevant issues in print culture are being challenged in digital culture. IFLA's 21 September 2005 Position on Internet Governance, for example, states:

> IFLA opposes any measures which would lead to control of information access and free expression by commercial, governmental

or sectoral interests. Measures which may be necessary to ensure reliable operation of the Internet, control spam, support intellectual property protection and enable individuals to protect their privacy must not be used to limit the rights expressed in the Universal Declaration of Human Rights, especially those in Article 19.[58]

On the subject of early twenty-first century security, accuracy and integrity of systems and data, Martha Smith writes:

> seeking social consensus rather than legal remedies may be the most effective approach. Firewalls, encryption technology, and government regulation may discourage encroachments but inequities of access and resources may aggravate competing or disadvantaged parties to risk sanctions in order to free captive knowledge ... there is the need to negotiate among all potential stakeholders ... cultivating community and striving for tolerance and mutual regard across cultures and regions, although seemingly idealistic, may be the most practical approach to security.[59]

Oral culture is also under siege. The National Library of Uganda's African Copyright Forum Project report titled 'Africa's Copyright Landscape', indicates that individual 'ownership of intellectual property was never part of the social and cultural fabrics of the traditional African society' and that 'the current international intellectual property rights regime grounded in western utilitarian school[s] presents real challenges to traditional African perspectives of intellectual property'. This is because:

> without resolving conflicts in perspectives, African countries are required to adopt western copyright regimes under the new Trade-Related Aspects of Intellectual Property Rights (TRIPS) agreement and other international agreements under the World Intellectual Property Rights Organization (WIPO) and the World Trade Organization (WTO).[60]

This culturally loaded terrain has direct implications for twenty-first century library-based knowledge practices, given that 'tracking in a library catalogue is very different than tracking in a digital world', and that collective memory represents more than 'recorded texts' and 'static' knowledge. These challenges and other dissonant collisions of culture have prompted interest in the emergent fields of intercultural information ethics and global information justice.

The issues expressed in this chapter frame an urgent and complex context for twenty-first century librarianship. The next chapter summarises basic treatments of information ethics and global information justice and links them to the concept of human rights and its contestations. The intention of this conceptual treatment is to set a path towards examining the moral responsibilities of library and information workers in the twenty-first century.

Notes

1. The International Federation of Library Associations and Institutions (IFLA) 'is the leading international body representing the interests of library and information services and their users. It is the global voice of the library and information profession. IFLA was founded in Edinburgh, Scotland, in 1927 and now has approximately 1700 members in 150 countries around the world. IFLA was registered in the Netherlands in 1971. The Royal Library, the national library of the Netherlands, in The Hague, generously provides the facilities for its headquarters.' (IFLA (2006) 'About IFLA'. Available at: *http://www.ifla.org/III/index.htm* (accessed 7 November 2006.))
2. Riedlmayer, A. (1996) 'Libraries are not for burning: international librarianship and the recovery of the destroyed heritage of Bosnia and Herzegovina', *INSPEL* 30(1): 82–3.
3. Ibid.
4. Esquivel, A. P. (2004) 'Between the walls of information and freedom', Proceedings of the 70th IFLA General Conference and Council, 22–27 August, Buenos Aires. Available at: *http://www.ifla.org/IV/ifla70/ps-Perez_Esquivel-e.htm* (accessed 8 November 2006).
5. Wiegand, W. A. (1999) 'Tunnel vision and blind spots: what the past tells us about the present; reflections on the twentieth-century history of American librarianship'. *Library Quarterly* 69(1): 24.
6. Andersen, A. (2005) 'Information criticism: Where is it?' *Progressive Librarian* Issue 25: 7.
7. Civallero, E. (2004) 'Indigenous libraries, utopia and reality: proposing an Argentine model', Aboriginal Libraries Project. National University, Córdoba.
8. Berman, S. (2005) 'Classism in the stacks', Jean E. Coleman Library Outreach Lecture, American Library Association. Available at: *http://www.ala.org/ala/olos/outreachresource/servicespoor.htm* (accessed 8 November 2006).
9. Ibid.
10. Ibid.
11. Capurro, R. (1992) 'What is information science for? A philosophical reflection', In Peter Vakkari and Blaise Cronin (eds) *Conceptions of Library and Information Science: Historical, Empirical and Theoretical*

Perspectives, London: Taylor Graham, pp. 90–3.

12. From: 'annette de faveri' *<annetdef@vpl.ca>*. To: *toni.samek@ualberta.ca*. Subject: Petition: CLA Interest Group. Date: 16 May 2006. LIBRARIES IN COMMUNITIES. TERMS OF REFERENCE.

13. Schiller, H. I. (1996) *Information Inequality: The Deepening Social Crisis in America*, New York: Routledge, p. 36.

14. Ibid., 37.

15. Pawley, C. (1998) 'Hegemony's handmaid? The library and information studies curriculum from a class perspective', *Library Quarterly* 68(2): 137.

16. Ibid., 123.

17. Ibid., 132.

18. Ibid., 139.

19. Blanke, H. T. (1989) 'Librarianship and political values: neutrality or commitment?', *Library Journal* 14 (July): 39–43.

20. Kagan, A. (2001) 'Living in the real world: a decade of progressive librarianship in the USA and in international library organizations', *Innovation* 22 (June): 11.

21. Ibid., 6–9.

22. Call for papers: 2005 Library History Seminar XI: Libraries in Times of War, Revolution & Social Change. Sponsored by the Library History Round Table of the American Library Association (ALA). Available at: *http://www.lis.uiuc.edu/conferences/LHS.XI/papers.pdf* (accessed 8 November 2006).

23. School of Library and Information Studies, University of Alberta, May 2005 draft of vision and mission.

24. Capurro, R. and Hjørland, B. (2003) 'The concept of information', *Annual Review of Information Science and Technology* 37: 389.

25. Caidi, N. (2005) Call for Papers: Special Issue of *Government Information Quarterly* on 'National Security Policies and Implications for Information Flow'.

26. Ibid.

27. Rosenzweig, M. (2001) 'What progressive librarians believe: an international perspective', *Innovation* 22 (June): 5.

28. Wiegand, S. (1996) 'Reality bites: the collision of rhetoric, rights, and reality and the Library Bill of Rights', *Library Trends* 45(1): 83.

29. Smith, M. (2001) 'Global information justice: rights, responsibilities, and caring connections', *Library Trends* 49(3): 534.

30. American Library Association (1997) 'Resolution on IFLA, human rights and freedom of expression'. Available at: *http://www.ala.org/ala/iro/awardsactivities/resolutionifla.htm* (accessed 8 November 2006).

31. Raseroka, K. (2004) World Library and Information Congress opening address, 70th IFLA General Conference and Council, 22–27 August, Buenos Aires, p. 2.

32. UNESCO (year unknown) 'Cultural diversity in the era of globalization'. Available at: *http://portal.unesco.org/culture/en/ev.php-URL_ID= 11605&URL_DO=DO_TOPIC&URL_SECTION=201.html* (accessed 8 November 2006).

33. Froehlich, T. J. (2000) 'Intellectual freedom, ethical deliberation and codes

of ethics', *IFLA Journal* 26: 4.

34. International Federation of Library Associations and Institutions (2005) 'More about IFLA: core values'. Available at: *http://www.ifla.org/III/intro00.htm* (accessed 8 November 2006).

35. International Federation of Library Associations and Institutions (1999) 'IFLA Statement on Libraries and Intellectual Freedom'. Statement prepared by IFLA/FAIFE and approved by The Executive Board of IFLA 25 March 1999, The Hague. Available at: *http://www.ifla.org/faife/policy/iflastat/iflastat.htm (accessed 8 November 2006).*

36. Duranni, S. (2004) Submission to Culture, Media and Sport Committee. Session 2003–04; 26 October. New Inquiry: Public Libraries. 19 November, p. 1.

37. IFLA Committee on Free Access to Information and Freedom of Expression (FAIFE) 'Annual Report 2003', p. 12. Available at: *www.ifla.org/faife/faife/ar2003.htm* (accessed 8 November 2006).

38. IFLA/UNESCO (1994) 'Public Library Manifesto'. Available at: *http://www.ifla.org/VII/s8/unesco/eng.htm* (accessed 8 November 2006).

39. UNESCO (2006) 'Human Rights Research'. Available at: *http://portal.unesco.org/shs/en/ev.php-URL_ID=3515&URL_DO=DO_TOPIC&URL_SECTION=201.html* (accessed 8 November 2006).

40. IFLA/FAIFE (2005) Launch of the IFLA/FAIFE World Report 2005. Media release, 16 August. Available at: *http://www.ifla.org/faife/report/WorldReport-pr-2005.htm* (accessed 8 November 2006).

41. Raseroka, K. (2005) 'Strategic plan for IFLA President's Report', World Library and Information Congress: 71st IFLA General Conference and Council, 14–18 August, Oslo, p. 6.

42. Listserv posting. From *shiraz.durrani@blueyonder.co.uk*. To: *lib-pikc@yahoogroups.com*. Date: 3 July 2004. Subject: Social Forum, Documentation and Libraries deadline.

43. Declaration from Buenos Aires on Information, Documentation and Libraries, 28 August, 2004. First Social Forum on Information, Documentation and Libraries: alternative action programs from Latin America for the information society, 26–28 August, Buenos Aires, called by the Social Studies Group on Library Science and Documentation (Argentina) and the Study Circle on Political and Social Librarianship (Mexico).

44. Ibid.

45. Listserv posting. From: *kellypw@umich.edu*. To: *pam@jeffersoncountylibrary.org*. Date: 31 May 2005. Subject: FW: IFRT New Orleans Program 2006.

46. Hazen, D. (2004) 'National bibliography in a globalized world: the Latin American case'. World Library and Information Congress: 70th IFLA General Conference and Council, 22–27 August, Buenos Aires, p. 4.

47. Listserv posting. From: *shiraz.durrani@blueyonder.co.uk*. To: *eddyobp2000@yahoo.co.uk*. Date: 19 Feb 2005. Subject: RE: AFRICA LIBERATION LIBRARY PROJECT – EXPRESSION OF INTEREST. Appeared in PLGNET-L Digest 2056.

48. Declaration from Buenos Aires on Information, Documentation and Libraries, op. cit.

49. UNESCO, op. cit.

50. Ibid.
51. Ibid.
52. Ibid.
53. Capurro, R. (1990) 'Towards an information ecology'. In: I. Wormell (ed.) *Information Quality. Definitions and Dimensions*, London: Taylor Graham, pp. 122–39.
54. Ibid.
55. UNESCO (2005) 'Knowledge versus information societies: UNESCO report takes stock of the difference'. Available at: *http://tinyurl.com/7mktr* and *http://unesdoc.unesco.org/images/0014/001418/141843e.pdf* (accessed 8 November 2006).
56. Ibid.
57. Information for Social Change (date unknown) 'Who are we?' Available at: *http://libr.org/isc/who.html* (accessed 8 November 2006).
58. International Federation of Library Associations and Institutions (2005) 'Position on Internet Governance'. Available at: *http://www.ifla.org/III/wsis/InternetGovernance.html* (accessed 8 November 2006).
59. Smith, M. (2001) 'Global information justice: rights, responsibilities, and caring connections,' *Library Trends* 49(3): 529.
60. National Library of Uganda (2005) 'The African Copyright Forum Project. Africa's Copyright Landscape'. Available at: *http://www.nlu.go.ug/acfc.htm#acl* (accessed 8 November 2006).
61. Good, K., Harder, G. and Binkley, P. (2005). 'Social bookmarking and wikis'. NEOS mini-conference, 3 June, Edmonton, Alberta. Available at: *http://www.neoslibraries.ca/content.aspx?p=592* (accessed 8 November 2006).

2

Human rights, contestations and moral responsibilities of library and information workers

This chapter proposes basic treatments of human rights (and their contestations), information ethics and global information justice. The concise and accessible treatments are presented at an introductory level. They are designed to act as a practical guidebook, not an academic text, and are intended as starting points to lay the foundation in support of ethical thinking on the moral responsibilities of library and information workers. This chapter supports the International Center for Information Ethics' (ICIE) open-ended stance that *some* of the articles in the Universal Declaration of Human Rights (1948) are 'a basis for ethical thinking on the responsibility of information specialists' and that 'information specialists have a moral responsibility with regard to the users at a micro (individuals), meso (institutions) and macro (society) level'.[1] The numerous strategies for social action documented in the second part of this book were selected because of their connection to elements of the Universal Declaration of Human Rights (1948) that relate particularly to core library values, information ethics, and global information justice. These elements include (but are not limited to):

- respect for the dignity of human beings (Art. 1);
- confidentiality (Art. 1, 2, 3, 6);
- equality of opportunity (Art. 2, 7);
- privacy (Art. 3, 12);
- right to be protected from torture or cruel, inhuman or degrading treatment or punishment (Art. 5);
- right to own property (Art. 17);

- right to freedom of thought, conscience and religion (Art. 18);
- right to freedom of opinion and expression (Art. 19);
- right to peaceful assembly and association (Art. 20);
- right to economic, social and cultural rights indispensable for dignity and the free development of personality (Art. 22);
- right to education (Art. 26);
- right to participate in the cultural life of the community (Art. 27);
- right to the protection of the moral and material interests concerning any scientific, literary or artistic production (Art. 27).[2]

The reader is also encouraged to pay attention to links between library and information work and the following three rights 'not yet incorporated into any legally-binding human rights instruments':[3]

- the right to communicate;
- the right to natural resources;
- the right to participation in mankind's heritage.

The Universal Declaration of Human Rights was adopted by the United Nations General Assembly in 1948. Although the Declaration is not a legally binding instrument, it directs member nations to advocate for numerous human, civil, economic and social rights. It establishes these rights as key conditions for freedom, justice and peace in the world. However, the United Nations' efforts to adopt a legally binding version of the Declaration were never realised because of disagreements and irreconcilable differences in opinion between a number of the member states about the acceptability of various rights. As a result, two separate covenants were developed to form an annex to the Declaration. Both the International Covenant on Civil and Political Rights and the International Covenant on Economic, Social and Cultural Rights were opened for signature in 1966 and entered into force in 1976. These two covenants are binding only with those member states that ratify them.

The following three parts comprise The International Bill of Human Rights:

- the Universal Declaration of Human Rights;
- the International Covenant on Economic, Social and Cultural Rights;
- the International Covenant on Civil and Political Rights and its two optional protocols. (The first optional protocol, adopted by the same

resolution, provides international machinery for communications from individuals who claim to be victims of violations of any of the rights set forth in the Covenant. The second optional protocol aims at the abolition of the death penalty and was adopted by the General Assembly in 1989.)

Other conventions have been developed over the years to complement the Universal Declaration of Human Rights (1948) and to address particular rights pertaining to such subjects as genocide, torture, racial discrimination, discrimination against women, children's rights, migrant workers and international criminal court.[4] The United Nations lists a total of seven core international human rights treaties. These are:[5]

- International Convention on the Elimination of All Forms of Racial Discrimination (21 December 1965);
- International Covenant on Civil and Political Rights (16 December 1966);
- International Covenant on Economic, Social and Cultural Rights (16 December 1966);
- Convention on the Elimination of All Forms of Discrimination against Women (18 December 1979);
- Convention against Torture and Other Cruel, Inhuman or Degrading Treatment or Punishment (10 December 1984);
- Convention on the Rights of the Child (20 Nov 1989);
- International Convention on the Protection of the Rights of All Migrant Workers and Members of Their Families (18 December 1990).

Expert committees monitor implementation of the treaty provisions by its signatories. Some treaties are supplemented by optional protocols. These are:

- Optional Protocol to the International Covenant on Civil and Political Rights (16 December 1966);
- Second Optional Protocol to the International Covenant on Civil and Political Rights, aiming at the abolition of the death penalty (15 December 1989);
- Optional Protocol to the Convention on the Elimination of Discrimination against Women (10 December 1999);
- Optional Protocol to the Convention on the Rights of the Child on the involvement of children in armed conflict (25 May 2000);

- Optional Protocol to the Convention on the Rights of the Child on the sale of children, child prostitution and child pornography (25 May 2000);
- Optional Protocol to the Convention against Torture and Other Cruel, Inhuman or Degrading Treatment or Punishment (18 December 2002).

In addition to the International Bill of Rights and the core human rights treaties, there are numerous other existing 'universal' instruments relating to human rights. For example, the World Conference on Human Rights, held at Vienna in June 1993, adopted by acclamation the Vienna Declaration and Programme of Action, which welcomes progress made in the codification of human rights instruments and urges the universal ratification of human rights treaties. In September 2000, the United Nations Millennium Declaration was adopted to reaffirm 'faith in the Organization and its Charter as indispensable foundations of a more peaceful, prosperous and just world'.[6] The Johannesburg Principles on National Security, Freedom of Expression and Access to Information (1996) underscores the relationship between information and human rights and helps serve as a point of reference of what constitutes information rights. Other 'universal' instruments apply to the:

- right to self-determination;
- rights of indigenous peoples and minorities;
- the prevention of discrimination;
- rights of women;
- rights of the child;
- rights of older persons;
- rights of persons with disabilities;
- human rights in the administration of justice and the protection of persons subjected to detention and imprisonment;
- social welfare, progress and development;
- promotion and protection of human rights;
- marriage;
- right to health;
- right to work and to fair conditions of employment;
- freedom of association;

- slavery, slavery-like practices and forced labour;
- rights of migrants;
- nationality, statelessness, asylum and refugees;
- war crimes and crimes against humanity, including genocide;
- humanitarian law.

In 1979, Karel Vasek proposed a taxonomy of three generations of human rights. The first-generation of human rights focuses on 'civil and political rights (right to life and political participation)'. The second generation of human rights emphasises 'economic, social and cultural rights (the right to subsistence)'.[7] The third generation highlights 'solidarity rights' which include the right to self-determination, to economic development, to social development, to natural resources, to communicate, and to participation in mankind's heritage. These latter rights are briefly covered in the International Covenant on Civil and Political Rights, 'but these provisions are an exceptional addition to the documents, which generally conceive of rights as an individual's claim upon society. This third generation has not yet been incorporated into any legally-binding human rights equivalent'.[8]

Furthermore, human rights theorists have challenged Vasek's taxonomy on the grounds that all rights are intextricably linked. UNESCO's Statement on Human Rights Research, for example, emphasises 'the promotion and protection of economic, social and cultural rights, especially the right to education, the right to take part in cultural life and the right to enjoy the benefits of scientific progress and its applications'.[9] It stresses 'the indivisibility, interdependence, interrelation and equal importance of all human rights (civil, cultural, economic, political and social)'.[10]

It is important to note the United Nation's qualification that:

> [the] legal status of these [its human rights] instruments varies: declarations, principles, guidelines, standard rules and recommendations have no binding legal effect, but such instruments have an undeniable moral force and provide practical guidance to States in their conduct; covenants, statutes, protocols and conventions are legally-binding for those States that ratify or accede to them.[11]

Always at issue is the number and relative importance of the countries ratifying the above instruments. The Office of the High Commissioner for Human Rights document titled 'Fact Sheet No.2 (Rev.1), The International Bill of Human Rights'[12] states that the Universal Declaration on Human Rights 'inspired the preparation of a number of international human rights instruments, both within and outside the United Nations system'; 'exercised a significant influence on a number of multilateral and bilateral treaties'; and 'had a strong impact as the basis for the preparation of many new national constitutions and national laws'. According to the Fact Sheet, the Declaration 'came to be recognized as a historic document articulating a common definition of human dignity and values', and is 'a yardstick by which to measure the degree of respect for, and compliance with, international human rights standards everywhere on earth'. Furthermore:

> [the] coming into force of the Covenants, by which States parties accepted a legal as well as a moral obligation to promote and protect human rights and fundamental freedoms, did not in any way diminish the widespread influence of the Universal Declaration. On the contrary, the very existence of the Covenants, and the fact that they contain the measures of implementation required to ensure the realization of the rights and freedoms set out in the Declaration, gives greater strength to the Declaration. The Universal Declaration is truly universal in scope. It preserves its validity for every member of the human family, everywhere, regardless of whether or not Governments have formally accepted its principles or ratified the Covenants. On the other hand, the Covenants, by their nature as multilateral conventions, are legally binding only on those States which have accepted them by ratification or accession.[13]

Not everyone agrees with this interpretation. As Gary Teeple argues in his book *The Riddle of Human Rights*:

> human rights as spelled out in The Universal Declaration of Human Rights are not *human rights* – that is, they are not elemental, inherent, or universal, but rather time-bound and relative to a particular mode of production. To be sure, they are a set of rights with a certain reality, but the qualifier 'human' obfuscates the relativity. The existence and concept of human rights are quintessentially ideological: they take what is and assert that as the truth.[14]

Consequently, 'although declared as absolutes', human rights 'have, from the beginning, been the subject of considerable conflict over interpretation and enforcement. They cannot be said, moreover, ever to have been wholly respected or upheld'. Martha Smith, for example, identifies contestation in that, the 'core information right affirmed' by the Declaration is:

> the protection of intellectual property with the sub-theme of social benefit. Even within Western capitalistic countries where individual property rights are taken very seriously this is not a universal value. Individuals with easy access to digital information, such as music on the Internet, are challenging traditional notions as to who owns what … Some would argue that it is impossible to stop the free flow of information in a digital age, so we might as well find ways to move beyond concepts such as copyrights and patents.[15]

Smith also suggests that:

> education dominated by commercial interests or by the English language may threaten vulnerable local languages and cultures. The right to education and the freedom to learn should go together with education for social responsibility and caring connections in the international quest for peace. Building community in the global information environment is sometimes associated with information democracy. But the idea of information democracy, like the digital divide, is a term that suggests noble aims but may conceal a subtle elitist utilitarianism that is self-serving for a small powerful minority.[16]

In effect, numerous criticisms of the Universal Declaration of Human Rights (1948) make it difficult to realise a consensus for 'universal' human rights.[17] Three common areas of concern are outlined below.

First, the Declaration implies a civic and political rather than a cultural emphasis. Second, the Declaration is inadequate in its protection of indigenous peoples, minorities, women, children and other disenfranchised groups. Third, the Declaration was developed to protect human rights in Western, autonomous, developed countries, and as a result is ineffectual in addressing human rights issues in developing nations. The south, for example, is unwilling to implement a declaration that is so contextually unsuitable.[18] In summary, the 'aspects of human rights most often attacked as Western are its individualism, its abstractness, and the concept of rights itself'.[19] Cultural diversity itself (with its plethora of divergent values, traditions, cultures and ways of being and knowing) must be accorded equal treatment in order to make way for the development of human rights that expand civil and political conceptions, that address cultural identity and difference, that take into account the gendered nature of societies, and that address the fact that 'transnational corporations unlike state governments do not sign international treaties defining and protecting human rights, and therefore are not accountable for violations of human rights'.[20] But even then it must be recognised that human rights are not absolutes and that there exist issues of higher magnitude, such as sustainable development and peace.

Philosophers in the overlapping fields of intercultural information ethics and global information justice articulate the strongest cases for linking library and information work to issues of human rights and sustainable development and peace. In Germany, in 1999, under the direction of Rafael Capurro, these philosophers formed an international collaborative scholarly community under the umbrella organisation called the International Center for Information Ethics.[21] The Center 'started as a small group of friends and colleagues but soon developed into an international and intercultural platform' that now draws more than 180 members from all over the world.[22]

Information ethics emerged as a concept in the library and information literature in the late 1980s, when both Robert Hauptman in the USA and Rafael Capurro in Germany 'used the term independently'.[23] According to Hauptman, information ethics can be understood as the point where 'the creation, discovery, dissemination, and application of information intersects with ethical considerations'.[24] In pushing for information ethics, Hauptman cautioned library and information workers: 'information is power. Uncontrolled information corrupts. That is why ethical considerations must mediate as one accumulates, accesses, or applies what one knows'.[25] Martha Smith asserts:

> Information ethics is concerned with the ethical conflicts and issues that arise in the use of information, information technologies, and information systems ... information ethics derives its topics from the choices and the decisions that must be made between competing interests using information systems. Major topics such as access, ownership, privacy, security, and democracy cover a multitude of dilemmas faced by information professionals and by the public.[26]

Rafael Capurro's evolving exploration of information ethics led him to develop the complementary idea of an *information ecology*, which applied to the context of this book, urges library and information workers to practise 'the art of friendship in the face of power'.[27] At present, information ethicists around the world are increasingly involved in the 'open task study of information ethics within different cultural traditions, i.e. what can be called intercultural information ethics'.[28]

Soraj Hongladarom and Charles Ess note, 'there is an urgent need for investigations into what the non-Western intellectual traditions have to say on the various issues in information ethics'.[29] Also receiving increased attention is the question of how 'globalization is providing indigenous peoples and indigenous knowledge and ways of being with new challenges'[30] (e.g. commodification as well as Edgardo Civallero's model proposal for indigenous libraries in Argentina[31]). In her discussion of the Inuvialuit of Sachs Harbour in Canada's Western Artic, Rosemarie Kuptana notes, 'Inuit Indigenous is an oral culture and cannot be written. To remove it from this oral context is to remove its meaning'.[32] This culturally loaded terrain has direct implications for twenty-first century library-based knowledge practices.

The ICIE website cautions: 'Classification systems, thesauri, search engines and the like are not neutral. This non-neutrality exists not only in their inherent bias but in the fact that specific unethical prejudices are not recognized, or acknowledged'.[33] Feminist library scholar Hope Olson, author of the book *The Power to Name: Locating the Limits of Subject Representation in Libraries*, concurs.[34] She observes:

> bias in subject access, whether subject headings, thesauri, or classification, is not just about the concepts that are represented or the terms used for them or even how things are grouped. It is even more culturally specific than that. The very structure of our systems is based on western logic ingrained in our culture since at least Aristotle. So when we export our systems (even with the best intentions) we are imposing our cultural model. It fits some cultures, but the primacy of hierarchy in our structures is a mismatch for other cultures. This frequently is the case with indigenous cultures among others. [Furthermore,] the current dominance of a single model for library cataloguing is a misunderstanding of the idea of standardization. When the idea of standardization is linked to the idea of sharing we end up with a homogenized product. With cataloging, this product ends up being based in western culture,

distributed through the efficiency of American corporate culture (e.g. OCLC [Online Computer Library Center]).[35]

Olson also observes that:

> subject access standards are what we use when naming information (e.g. subject headings, thesauri, how we connect concepts and the terms that represent them, and how we group and juxtapose concepts in classification). Because naming is a way of wielding power whether intentionally or not it is also an opportunity for fostering social change. If we control the language of naming we influence social change.[36]

She predicts 'we will never have bias-free subject access and that isn't necessarily a bad thing. What is important is that we are aware of our biases (some of which ARE inappropriate anywhere) and of the power we're exercising'.[37] She suggests 'we can use standards (like controlled vocabularies) without locking ourselves into some monolithic view ... use options and adaptations'.[38] Finally, borrowing from Ursula Franklin, Olson asserts, 'technology can facilitate the viability of local options or adaptations for particular sectors'.[39] In a similar vein, Sanford Berman has been improving upon cumbersome, impractical, outdated, and inhumane subject headings of the Library of Congress since the 1960s.[40] His groundbreaking treatment of demographic differences in subject headings and classification in Hennepin County (Minnesota) Library's online catalogue has been used as an alternative to the subject headings of the Library of Congress.[41] Olson's, Berman's, and others' critical library work blends seamlessly with the warnings carried by information ethicists. Rafael Capurro and Birger Hjørland, for example, caution that:

> [as] information systems become more global and interconnected, implicit information is often lost. This situation challenges information science to be more responsive to the social and cultural impacts of interpretive processes as well as the qualitative differences between different contexts and media. This challenge means including interpretive processes as a *conditio sine qua non* of information processes.[42]

California-based Internet search engine Google's massive digitisation project has prompted contentious debate about the company's for-profit status, the need for democratic access to the Information Commons, Anglo-American cultural dominance, and copyright. Led by the protest of Jean-Noël Jeanneney, President of the Bibliothèque Nationale de France, a counter 'European digital library' is now under discussion, in what is termed the 'future geography of knowledge'.[43] By 1 June 2005, approximately 23 national libraries in the EU's 25 member states had expressed the desire for a European search engine.[44] Within this context, it is necessary to consider how cultural workers will be able to participate in 'the conscious and unconscious cultural biases that silence alternative viewpoints and erase the experiences of ethnic and cultural groups from the historical record, so that inconvenient, or embarrassing or terrible events can be glossed over, denied or forgotten'.[45]

Closely related to intercultural information ethics is *global information justice*. Building on Capurro's foundational work, such as 'What is information science for? A philosophical reflection', Smith coined the phrase 'global information justice' in 2001 in a groundbreaking paper titled 'Global information justice: rights, responsibilities, and caring connections'.[46] 'The goal of global information justice (GIJ)' she writes, 'is to conserve nature and to preserve humanity through the creative uses of the technologies of information, knowledge, and memory using the practices of rights, responsibilities and caring connections'.[47] Since 2001, GIJ has been developing as an international discipline committed to guiding library and information workers and 'global policy makers and to informing and empowering citizens of the world'.[48] Key aspects of GIJ integral to informing this book are excerpted here:

- 'GIJ assumes that cultural differences shape the ways that various people relate to information and its role in society. Nevertheless, GIJ also posits the ideals of the Universal Declaration of Human Rights as worthy goals in moving toward a practical international consensus on issues such as intellectual property rights. GIJ accepts the claims of conflicting local and national systems but calls on all parties to move beyond law to promote world relationships of sharing and mutual responsibilities for the natural world and for human welfare'.[49]

- 'Like the ideals in the Universal Declaration of Human Rights, the ideal of global information justice calls for attitudes and actions that are hard to achieve. Implementation is only possible if individuals, groups, institutions, and nations are able to go beyond law and rights and move to mutual responsibility and caring concern. The practical basis for this affirmation is concern for survival of the planet and all living beings, including animals, plants, and potentially sentient machines'.[50]

- 'GIJ enlarges the analytical space for considering claims beyond the legal rights of the favored party. Accepting some measure of social responsibility for all humanity and nature takes one step beyond entitlement'.[51]

- 'The theme of global information justice runs through the Universal Declaration of Human Rights and can be appreciated in the twenty-first century even more than it was fifty years ago. Privacy, information transfer across borders, free exchange of ideas, protection of intellectual property, and the right to know everything – from ones' own genetic blueprint to someone else's criminal record – are among the issues that need to need to be addressed with respect to diverse values and competing interests'.[52] Martha Smith observes that like the words of the Universal Declaration of Human Rights (1948):

> the words of UNESCO may seem to be weak weapons when up against corporate capitalism, environmental degradation, and the chaos of war and poverty. However, in the long run, words may be able to exert the force of conscience on a wired planet where conflicts may not be amenable to conflicting value systems and competing laws and armies.[53]

The challenge, of course, is in realising human rights' ideals and abstractions in actual realities such as the amelioration of social problems. Gary Teeple observes, 'many thousands of organizations and millions of people are dedicated to defending, advancing, and clarifying' human rights 'within an accelerating struggle to have human rights respected and an accompanying expansion in consciousness about their nature and violations'. Furthermore, 'despite continuous violations and systematic obfuscation and rationalization of the violations, the demand for these rights and the consciousness surrounding their nature continue to grow'.[54] Part of this insistence and awareness is about library and information work. For example, the 2004 workbook, *New Tactics in Human Rights: A Resource for Practitioners* includes specific human rights tactics for library and information work.[55] These include:

- 'Empowering children with information, skills and support to advocate for their own rights.'[56]

- Empowering people with information skills 'to use the legal system to exert their rights.'[57]

- 'Protecting freedom of thought and the right to privacy by destroying records that could be demanded by the government.'[58]

- 'Building effective libraries and employing librarians to effectively provide information support to advocates and activists.'[59]

- 'Protecting cultural and economic rights of indigenous people by recording traditional ecological knowledge [and protecting it from exploitative patents].'[60]

- 'Mapping personal histories and mobilizing memory to reclaim a place in history and recover lost land.'[61]

- 'Coordinating efforts to preserve archival information among several organizations and creating a system for accessing it.'[62]

- 'Promoting justice by leveraging the legal rights to access victims' records (e.g. in Paraguay, former prisoners have the legal right to control documents related to their own cases – these are digitized to create an "archive of terror").'[63]

- 'Documenting records of abuse to promote healing and justice.'[64]

- 'Identifying allies to hold constructive dialogue and maintain cooperative relationships.'[65]

The second part of this book presents existing examples of how library and information workers worldwide are using creative forms of empowerment to address the continuing need for recognition and representation, the ongoing battle against social exclusion, and those conflicts that have resulted from failures to acknowledge human rights. Taken as a whole, the examples represent a compelling chorus of voices (at times harmonious, other times fractious) blending library and information work into the global discourse of human rights and its contestations. The applicability of each of the strategies is dependent on the reader's individual contexts. It is of paramount importance for the reader to consider that the practice of critical librarianship in the twenty-first century is an option that individual library and information workers can choose or not. Many library and information workers who struggle against innumerable forms of oppression do so with the knowledge that they are making a difference in people's lives, and not with the expectation of any tangible reward. It is the hope of this author that this book will be used by library and information workers not only as a guide that informs their critical thinking on library and information work in the twenty-first century, but as a practical tool that provides library and information workers with concrete strategies for implementing changes in their individual and collective spheres of influence'.[66] This author, for one, supports Herbert I. Schiller's assertion that 'making a difference that counts in the information-cultural situation depends on political action'.[67]

Notes

1. International Center for Information Ethics (2006) 'The field: 3.1 Human rights and responsibility'. Available at: *http://icie.zkm.de/research* (accessed 8 November 2006).
2. UNESCO (1948) Universal Declaration of Human Rights. Available at: *http://www.un.org/Overview/rights.html* (accessed 8 November 2006).
3. Wikipedia (2006) 'Three generations of human rights'. Available at: *http://en.wikipedia.org/wiki/Three_generations_of_human_rights* (accessed 15 February 2006).
4. For example, Convention on the Prevention and Punishment of the Crime of Genocide (entry into force: 1951); Convention against Torture (entry into force: 1984); Convention on the Elimination of All Forms of Racial Discrimination (entry into force: 1969); Convention on the Elimination of All Forms of Discrimination Against Women (entry into force: 1981); Convention on the Rights of the Child (entry into force: 1989); Rome Statute of the International Criminal Court (entry into force: 2002).
5. Office of the United Nations High Commissioner for Human Rights (year unknown) 'International law'. Available at: *http://www.ohchr.org/english/law/* (accessed 8 November 2006).
6. United Nations (2000) The United Nations Millennium Declaration. Available at: *http://www.ohchr.org/english/law/millennium.htm* (accessed 8 November 2006).
7. Ibid.
8. Wikipedia, op. cit.
9. UNESCO (2006) 'Human Rights Research'. Available at: *http://portal .unesco.org/shs/en/ev.php-URL_ID=3515&URL_DO=DO_TOPIC& URL_SECTION=201.html* (accessed 8 November 2006).
10. Ibid.
11. The Office of the High Commissioner for Human Rights (1996) 'Fact Sheet No.2 (Rev.1): The International Bill of Human Rights', Geneva: United Nations. Available at: *http://www.unhchr.ch/html/menu6/2/fs2.htm* (accessed 8 November 2006).
12. Ibid.
13. Ibid.
14. Teeple. G. (2004) *The Riddle of Human Rights*, Aurora, Ontario: Garamond Press, p. 1.

15. Smith, M. (2001) 'Global information justice: rights, responsibilities, and caring connections', *Library Trends* 49(3): 526–7.
16. Ibid., 539.
17. See for example, Bell, D. J. (1996) 'The East Asian challenge to human rights: reflections on an East-West dialogue', *Human Rights Quarterly* 18(3): 641–67; Bowring, W. (2002) 'Forbidden relations: The UK's discourse of human rights and the struggle for social justice', *Law, Social Justice & Global Development Journal* (1); Brems, E. (1997) 'Enemies or Allies? Feminism and cultural relativism as dissident voices in human rights discourse', *Human Rights Quarterly* 19(1): 136–64; Jamal, A. (2005) 'Transnational feminism as critical practice: a reading of feminist discourses in Pakistan', *Meridians: Feminism, Race, Transnationalism* 5(2): 57–82; Langlois, A. J. (2003) 'Human rights without democracy? A critique of the separationist thesis', *Human Rights Quarterly*, 25(4): 990–1019; Meyer, W. H. (1996) 'Human rights and MNCs: theory versus quantitative analysis', *Human Rights Quarterly* 18(2): 368–97; Oloka-Onyango, J. (2005) 'Who's watching "Big Brother"? Globalization and the protection of cultural rights in present day Africa', *Human Rights Quarterly* 27(4): 1245–73; Oloka-Onyango, J. and Tamale, S. (1995) '"The personal is political", or Why women's rights are indeed human rights: an African perspective on international feminism', *Human Rights Quarterly*, 17(4): 691–731; Smith, J., Bolyard, M. and Ippolito A. (1999) 'Human rights and the global economy: a response to Meyer', *Human Rights Quarterly* 21(1): 207–19; Stammers, N. (1999) 'Social movements and the social construction of human rights', *Human Rights Quarterly* 21(4): 980–1008; Visweswaran, K. (2004) 'Gendered state: rethinking culture as site of South Asian human rights work', *Human Rights Quarterly* 26(2): 483–511.
18. Thanks to Anna-Marie Klassen for her informative support in exploring human rights critiques.
19. Brems, op. cit., 145.
20. Smith et al., op. cit., 211.
21. International Center for Information Ethics (ICIE) website (*http://icie.zkm.de/*) (accessed 8 November 2006).
22. International Center for Information Ethics (2001) 'What is ICIE?' Available at: *http://icie.zkm.de/* (accessed 8 November 2006).
23. Hauptman, R. (1999) 'Information ethics', *Choice* 37(3): 261.
24. Ibid.
25. Ibid.
26. Ibid., 339.
27. Smith, M. M. (1997) 'Information ethics' in M. E. Williams (ed.) *Annual Review of Information Science and Technology*. Vol. 32, Medford, NJ: Information Today, Inc.; pp. 339–366.
28. International Center for Information Ethics (2006) 'The field'. Available at: *http://icie.zkm.de/research* (accessed 8 November 2006).
29. Call for chapters for S. Hongladarom and C. Ess (eds) *Information Technology Ethics: Cultural Perspectives*. Available at: *http://www3.iath.virginia.edu/lists_archive/Humanist/v18/0692.html* (accessed 30 April 2005).
30. Listserv posting. From: *makere@ualberta.ca*. To: *edfaculty@mailman.srv*

.ualberta.ca. Date: 9 May 2005. Subject: Fall grad course. EDPS 601. Indigenous Ontologies in the Global Context.

31. Civallero, E. (2004) 'Indigenous libraries, utopia and reality: proposing an Argentine model', *Proceedings of the 70th IFLA General Conference and Council*, 22–27 August, Buenos Aires. Available at: *http://eprints.rclis .org/archive/00003104/* (accessed 8 November 2006).

32. Kuptana, R. (2005) 'Relationship between traditional knowledge and intellectual cultural properties: an Inuit perspective', Discussion Paper, National Gatherings on Indigenous Knowledge, Canadian Heritage, Government of Canada, p. 2.

33. International Center for Information Ethics (2005) 'The field'. Available at: *http://icie.zkm.de/research* (accessed 8 November 2006).

34. Olson, H. A. (2002) *The Power to Name: Locating the Limits of Subject Representation in Libraries*, Dordrecht: Kluwer, p. 261.

35. In personal e-mail communication with Hope Olson (Professor, School of Information Studies, University of Wisconsin-Milwuakee). Further examples of Olson's leading work include: Olson, H. A. and Schlegl, R. (2001) 'Critiques of subject access bias: A meta-analysis', *Cataloging & Classification Quarterly* 32(2): 61–80; Olson, H. A. (2000) 'Difference, culture, and change: The untapped potential of LCSH', *Cataloging & Classification Quarterly* 29(1/2); and Olson, H. A. (2001) 'Sameness and difference: A cultural foundation of classification', *Library Resources & Technical Services* 45(3): 115–22.

36. Ibid.

37. Ibid.

38. See: Olson, H. A. and Ward, D. B. (2003) 'Subject retrieval in a networked environment', in M. McIlwaine (ed.) Proceedings of the IFLA Satellite Meeting, 14–16 August 2001, Dublin, OH; München: KG Saur, pp. 50–8.

39. Ibid.

40. See Berman, S. (1971) *Prejudices and Antipathies: A Tract on the LC Subject Heads Concerning People*, Metuchen, NJ: Scarecrow Press; and Berman, S. (1981) *The Joy of Cataloging: Essays, Letters, Reviews and Other Explosions*. Phoenix, AZ: Oryx Press.

41. Sanford Berman website. Available at: *http://www.sanfordberman.org/* (accessed 7 November 2006).

42. Capurro, R. and Hjørland B. (2003) 'The concept of information', *Annual Review of Information Science and Technology* Vol. 37; p. 397.

43. Listserv posting. From: *lib-plic@yahoogroups.com*. To: *lib-plic@ yahoogroups.com*. Date: 11 May 2005. Subject: Europe vs Google: EU proposes Digital Library to counter Google-US/UK-centric version. From the *LA Times* business section, 10 May, 2005.

44. Ibid.

45. Listserv posting. From: *kellypw@umich.edu*. To: *pam@jeffersoncountylibrary .org*. Date: 31 May 2005. Subject: FW: IFRT New Orleans Program 2006.

46. Smith, M. (2001) 'Global information justice: rights, responsibilities, and caring connections', *Library Trends* 49(3): 519–37.

47. Ibid., 520.

48. Ibid., 521.

49. Ibid., 534–5.
50. Ibid., 523.
51. Ibid.
52. Ibid., 521.
53. Ibid., 530–1.
54. Teeple, op. cit., 4.
55. The Center for Victims of Torture (2004) *New Tactics in Human Rights: A Resource Guide for Practitioners*, Minneapolis, MN: The Center for Victims of Torture.
56. Ibid., 143.
57. Ibid., 40.
58. Ibid., 45.
59. Ibid., 137.
60. Ibid., 46.
61. Ibid., 112.
62. Ibid., 89.
63. Ibid., 88.
64. Ibid., 87.
65. Ibid., 129.
66. Teeple, op. cit., 5.
67. Schiller, H. I. (1989) *Culture, Inc.: The Corporate Takeover of Public Expression*, New York: Oxford University Press, p. 168.

Part Two: The Reality

'Action expresses priorities'.
Mohandas Gandhi

3

Practical strategies for social action

Building librarianship on a solid foundation of human dignity, freedom, social justice and cultural diversity requires that library and information workers worldwide constantly and relentlessly tackle social, political, cultural, legal, economic, technological and ideological issues. It is relatively easy to identify the issues: all one has to do is pay attention to news of the world. Developing concrete strategies for tackling them, however, takes more effort, and that is what this part of this book addresses.

One of the explicit aims of the international activist group Information for Social Change (ISC) is to 'encourage information workers to come together, to share ideas,' and to develop alternatives.[1] Having joined the ISC Board, this author felt it only appropriate to share something along these lines. This work, then, is intended to be of practical help to library and information workers around the world who face broad issues they seek and/or have professional responsibility to negotiate in concrete terms at an individual, institutional, or societal level. These issues could include limited access to government information; heightened legalistic atmospheres; competing political, economic and ideological agendas; post-September 11 legislation, policy and practice; criminology in service of the state; suspect communities (e.g. Muslims, Asians, activists, protestors and dissenters); the nexus between universities, employers and the state; global market fundamentalism; the rise of corporate managerialism; pressures from private groups and government (e.g. as seen in Iran, Iraq, China, Egypt, Tunisia, Columbia, North Korea, India and former constituent republics of the USSR); climate of fear; self-censorship; implications of the World Trade Organization's GATS and TRIPS agreements; the contingent worker model; transborder data flow and limits to international exchange of ideas; risk assessment models; imposed technologies; global infrastructure of mass registration and surveillance; information poverty; and transmodification of speech into punishable action.

The practical guidance that follows is organised into two sections. The first briefly describes prevalent manifestations of social action applied directly to library and information work, followed by concrete examples of the strategies at play. The second section contains specific strategies for social action used in library and information work, again followed by concrete examples. In both sections, to preserve their integrity, the brief descriptions of each strategy are quoted or excerpted from the original voices. Most examples are contemporary, but a few older ones are included to contextualise present-day library activism in its historical context. Although many examples are from Canada and the USA, numerous other geopolitical contexts are represented in the examples, including Argentina, Australia, Bosnia, China, Cuba, Denmark, Germany, Hungary, Iraq, Kenya, Kosovo, Mali, Mexico, Nigeria, Spain, Sweden, Switzerland, Thailand, the UK, Vietnam, and Zimbabwe. Taken together, the examples highlight diversity in local, national and international library and information work.

A subtext of this work is the purposeful inclusion of and, hence, the de-marginalisation of, the agendas of numerous local, national and international library groups that readily identify themselves as progressive, critical, activist, radical, alternative, independent, socially responsible and/or anarchistic in orientation. Among these are the Anarchist Librarians Web, Arbeitskreis kritischer Bibliothekarinnen und Bibliothekare, Arbeitskreis kritischer BibliothekarInnen, Bibliotek i Samhälle, Cuban Libraries Solidarity Group, Círculode Estudios sobre Bibliotecología Política y Social, El Grupo de Estudios Sociales en Bibliotecología y Documentación, Information for Social Change, Librarians Without Borders, Progressive African Library and Information Activists' Group, Progressive Librarians Guild, Progressive Librarians' International Coalition, Radical Reference, and the Social Responsibilities Round Table of the American Library Association. Such groups represent various points on the continuum of library and information perspectives and are, therefore, sometimes complementary in their approach to issues, sometimes at odds in them. Ultimately, they demonstrate varying degrees of difference and commonality in their social action agendas. For example, although the Progressive Librarians' International Coalition identifies itself as an active, contemporary, international library network of progressive librarians who participate in 'exchanging views, submitting early warnings, sending signed petitions or other letters on urgent issues' that threaten libraries and intellectual freedom, participants 'don't have to share a common view on each library or social subject' and 'are not obliged to go along with every initiative on the list'. They do, however, share a common ground.[2]

The following ten points asserted by the Coalition are a starting place for understanding 'a basis of principles/goals shared worldwide by' critical librarians.[3] Readers are encouraged to refer to these points while working through the practical examples in the second section. In the process, it should become apparent that social action in the context of library and information work involves both so-called mainstream and progressive pushes. Whereas historically the western claim to library neutrality drew a line between library advocacy and library activism, this work will, hopefully, help to both blur that artificial line and to demystify social action in the profession. It is also hoped that the examples presented will demonstrate that social action via librarianship is both necessary and inherent in the very nature of the profession. Moreover, as borne out in the examples, many twenty-first century library and information workers who would not identify themselves as progressive, by virtue of their practice and defence of intellectual freedom and their promotion and use of libraries (especially public and school libraries) as public space, already contribute to social action on a daily basis.

The Progressive Librarians' International Coalition's Ten Points:[4]

1. We shall work towards an international agenda as the basis of common action of librarians everywhere actively committed, as librarians, to social justice, equality, human welfare and the development of cultural democracy.

2. We will unite librarians and information workers in opposition to the marketization of public goods, to privatization of social resources and to outsourcing of services and will oppose international treaties and institutions which advance destructive neo-liberal policies.

3. We insist upon the equality of access to and inclusiveness of information services, especially extending such services to the poor, marginalized and discriminated against, including the active solidarity-based provision of information assistance to these groups and their advocates in their struggles.

4. We shall encourage the exploration of alternative models of human services; promote and disseminate critical analysis of

information technology's impact on libraries and societies; and support the fundamental democratization of existing institutions of education, culture, communications.

5. We shall undertake joint, interdisciplinary research into fundamental library issues (e.g. into the political economy of information in the age of neo-liberalism and corporate globalization) in order to lay the basis for effective action in our spheres of work.

6. We will support cooperative collection, organization and preservation of the documents of people's struggles and the making available of alternative materials representing a wide range of progressive viewpoints often excluded as resources from the debates of our times.

7. We will investigate and organize efforts to make the library-as-workplace more democratic and encourage resistance to the managerialism of the present library culture.

8. We will lead in promoting international solidarity among librarians and cooperation between libraries across borders on the basis of our joint commitment to the Universal Declaration of Human Rights and related covenants which create a democratic framework for constructive cooperative endeavours.

9. We will organize in common with other cultural and educational progressives, to help put issues of social responsibility on the agendas of international bodies such as IFLA and UNESCO.

10. We shall oppose corporate globalization which, despite its claims, reinforces existing social, economic, cultural inequalities and insist on a democratic globalism and internationalism which respects and cultivates cultural plurality, which recognizes the sovereignty of peoples, which acknowledges the obligations of society to the individual and communities and which prioritizes human values and needs over profits.

Notes

1. Information for Social Change. 'Who are we?' Available at: *http://libr.org/isc/who.html* (accessed 8 November 2006).
2. BIS. (year unknown) 'The lib-plic list'. Available at: *http://www.foreningenbis.org/English/lib_plic.html* (accessed 8 November 2006).
3. Ibid.
4. Ibid.

Prevalent manifestations of social action applied to library and information work

In their new millennium activist guide *Global Uprising: Confronting the Tyrannies of the Twenty-First Century: Stories from a New Generation of Activists*, Neva Welton and Linda Wolf document prevalent manifestations of social action. A sampling of these manifestations is presented here in alphabetical order: anarchism, campaigns, cooperation, coalitions, infiltration, mass direct action, militancy, mobilisation, movement, non-violent direct action, organisation, refuge, resistance, revitalisation, solidarity, struggle and survival.[1] Here, each of these manifestations is applied to library and information work and clear, practical examples of their application are presented. It is important to note that the examples are not exhaustive or mutually exclusive and that they overlap. It is also important to note that the application of a particular manifestation to a given example is an interpretive and subjective process. As such, readers are encouraged to modify and develop the examples in consideration of the political, legal, economic, ideological, technological and cultural contexts of the countries and communities in which they live and labour, as well as more personal factors such as their own gender, class, sexual orientation, citizenship, disability, ethnic origin, geographical location, language, political philosophy, race or religion. The examples given below are intended to be starting points, not ending points.

Definitions of the manifestations of social action are derived from the following online resources:

- Online Dictionary for Library and Information Science (ODLIS): *http://lu.com/odlis/index.cfm*

- Oxford English Dictionary Online (OED): *http://www.oed.com/*
- Wikipedia – The Free Encyclopedia: *http://en.wikipedia.org/*

Sources of direct quotations are given at the end of each entry.

Anarchism

Definition

A theoretical social state in which there is no governing person or body of persons, but each individual has absolute liberty (without implication of disorder). (OED)

Examples

Anarchist Librarians Web

Anarchist Librarians Web is a 'network of radical and anarchist librarians who are working towards a better world and socially responsible libraries. We get together at library conventions, anarchist conferences and radical book fairs to put on protests, raise awareness, or simply drink beers together.'

Source: *http://www.infoshop.org/alibrarians/public_html* (accessed 8 November 2006).

Kate Sharpley Library

Named in honour of Kate Sharpley, a First World War anarchist, anti-war activist and one of the countless 'unknown' members of the movement so often ignored in 'official histories' of anarchism, the Library is dedicated to researching and restoring the history of the anarchist movement. It currently contains 'over 10,000 English language books, pamphlets and periodicals on anarchism, including complete or near complete runs of *Black Flag, Direct Action* (from 1945 onwards), *Freedom, Man, Spain and the World, Freedom* (USA), *Why, The Blast, Spanish Revolution* and a host of others'. It also has strong collections of 'posters, leaflets, manuscripts, letters and internal records, including reports from the IWA (AIT/IAA), the Anarchist Federation of Britain (1945–1950), the Syndicalist Workers Federation (1950–1979), Cienfuegos Press, ASP' and others. Its collection of materials in languages other than English includes similar materials, including 'many rare pamphlets and newspapers'.

Source: *http://katesharpleylibrary.net/* (accessed 7 November 2006).

Campaigns

Definition

Esp. in politics. An organised course of action designed to arouse public opinion throughout the country for or against some political object, or to influence the voting at an election of members of the legislature. (OED)

Example

Campaign for the World's Libraries

'The Campaign for the World's Libraries is a public education campaign of the International Federation of Library Associations and Institutions, the American Library Association and libraries around the world to speak loudly and clearly about the value of libraries and librarians in the twenty-first century. It is designed to showcase the unique and vital roles played by public, school, academic and special libraries worldwide.' The three core messages of the Campaign are (1) 'libraries are changing and dynamic places', (2) 'libraries are places of opportunity', and (3) 'libraries bridge the world'. Through the consistent delivery of these key messages, the campaign aims to 'raise awareness about the variety of programs and services offered; increase use of libraries at schools, at colleges and universities, in government, at work and in daily community life; increase funding for libraries; involve librarians as stakeholders on public policy issues such as intellectual freedom, equity of access and the "digital divide"'; and 'to encourage librarianship as a profession.'

Source: *http://www.ifla.org/@yourlibrary/* (accessed 8 November 2006).

Cooperation

Definition

The action of cooperating, i.e. of working together towards the same end, purpose or effect; joint operation. (OED)

Example

North-South library cooperation: some consideration

In this paper, presented to the IFLA Social Responsibilities Discussion Group, Abdullahi argues that the 'crisis through which international information and communication are now developing presents great dangers if the growing gap between the information rich North and the information poor South is not considered seriously'. The paper argues 'the introduction of electronic technology in the field of information studies is even further widening the dividing line between North and South'. A need is expressed to 'narrow this growing gap through cooperation of library and information service and through a common approach and dialogue' necessary to 'establish the trust relationship necessary for effective information sharing'. This dialogue, it is asserted, 'must provide every country the full potential development of infrastructure and access of information whenever and wherever it is needed'. The paper recommends 'strategies and ways these co-operations could be established'.

Source: Abdullahi, I. (1998) 'North-South library cooperation: some consideration'. Available at: *http://www.ifla.org/VII/dg/srdg/srdg4.htm* (accessed 7 November 2006).

Coalitions

Definition

Esp. in politics. An alliance for combined action of distinct parties, persons, or states, without permanent incorporation into one body. (OED)

Example

Canadian Coalition for School Libraries

'In March, 2002, a group of individuals and organizations founded the Canadian Coalition for School Libraries [CCSL], an alliance of parents, writers, academics, literacy advocates, public librarians, teacher-librarians, publishers, wholesalers and children's specialists ... The CCSL advocates well-funded, professionally-staffed school libraries as a means of improving student achievement. School library programs are being drastically reduced across the country as school boards confront funding shortfalls. But cuts are occurring when researchers abroad have determined that well-stocked, professionally-staffed school libraries which remain open during the day are linked to student achievement, reading, information literacy skills and success at the post-secondary level ... The CCSL is establishing provincial school library coalitions, composed of groups dedicated to promoting improved school library policies and funding. We are seeking funds to establish a national office to support provincial coalitions and promote re-investment in Canadian school libraries to the public, policy-makers and the media.'

Source: *http://www.peopleforeducation.com/librarycoalition/* (accessed 8 November 2006).

Infiltration

Definition

Fig., esp. for the purpose of political subversion. (OED)

Example

A Network Institute for Global Democratization 'Library Workshop' during the 2006 World Social Forum

The Network Institute for Global Democratization (NIGD) arranged for a two-day library workshop during the World Social Forum (WSF) in Bamako, Mali, 19–23 January 2006, on the 'role of the libraries in the WSF process'. The process included 'all the global, regional, national and local social forums since 2001'. Questions raised and answered included 'How to raise library-consciousness within the WSF-process; how to raise WSF-consciousness among the library and information professionals; dissemination of WSF-information via libraries: methods, practical solutions; documentation of the WSF in the public libraries; project strategies, organisation and funding'. An 'additional task' was to 'initiate the preparations of the library-related events at the WSF in Nairobi 2007.'

Source: *http://www.nigd.org/libraries/bamako-nairobi* (accessed 8 November 2006).

Mass direct action

Definition

Direct action is a form of political activism that seeks immediate remedy for perceived ills, as opposed to indirect actions, such as electing representatives who promise to provide remedy at some later date. Those employing direct action aim to either:

- obstruct another agent or organisation from performing some practice to which they object.
- act with whatever resources and methods are within their power, either on their own or as part of a group, in order to solve problems. (Wikipedia)

Examples

The American Library Association's (ALA) Resolution on the USA Patriot Act 2001

In January, 2003 ALA adopted its 'Resolution on the USA Patriot Act and Related Measures That Infringe on the Rights of Library Users'. Among other things, it resolved that the Association

1. 'encourages all librarians, library administrators, library governing bodies and library advocates to educate their users, staff and communities about the process for compliance with the USA Patriot

Act and other related measures and about the dangers to individual privacy and the confidentiality of library records resulting from those measures';

2. 'urges librarians everywhere to defend and support user privacy and free and open access to knowledge and information';

3. 'will work with other organizations, as appropriate, to protect the rights of inquiry and free expression';

4. 'will take actions as appropriate to obtain and publicize information about the surveillance of libraries and library users by law enforcement agencies and to assess the impact on library users and their communities';

5. 'urges all libraries to adopt and implement patron privacy and record retention policies that affirm that "the collection of personally identifiable information should only be a matter of routine or policy when necessary for the fulfillment of the mission of the library" (ALA Privacy: An Interpretation of the Library Bill of Rights) and considers that "sections of the USA Patriot Act are a present danger to the constitutional rights and privacy rights of library users"'.

The Resolution included a set of recommendations to 'be forwarded to the President of the United States, to the Attorney General of the United States, to Members of both Houses of Congress, to the library community and to others as appropriate'.

Source: *http://www.ala.org/ala/washoff/WOissues/civilliberties/ theusapatriotact/alaresolution.htm* (accessed 8 November 2006).

Another 'hysteric' librarian for freedom button

'The American Library Association (ALA) Office for Intellectual Freedom introduces a new product for the thousands of librarians who fight everyday to protect the privacy rights of library users. "Another 'Hysteric' Librarian for Freedom" button acknowledges this important work while referencing the recent misstatement by US Attorney General John Ashcroft ... For the last several months, the Attorney General has toured American cities, trying to drum up support for the USA PATRIOT Act, which gives law enforcement easy access to library records with minimal judicial oversight. In several of his speeches, he has described librarians—among the first to denounce portions of the Act as giving unprecedented powers of surveillance to the government, particularly in libraries—as "hysterics". To help raise awareness of the overreaching aspects of the USA Patriot Act, ALA's Office for Intellectual Freedom will sell the buttons ... All proceeds support the programs of the office'.

Source: *http://www.ala.org/ala/oif/basics/basicrelatedlinks/librarianfreedom.htm* (accessed 8 November 2006).

Militancy

Definitions

Militancy: The condition or fact of being militant, esp. (in later use) in pursuing a political or social end.

Militant: Aggressively active in pursuing a political or social cause and often favouring extreme, violent, or confrontational methods. (OED)

Examples

Cultural cleansing in the Balkans

The power that militancy through library and information work holds as a potential force of social change is perhaps best illustrated by the anti-militancy that librarians and libraries demonstrated during the cultural cleansing that occurred in the Balkans in the early 1990s. Alex Byrne, Chairman of the IFLA Committee on Free Access to Information and Freedom of Expression wrote that 'For us, the question is the responsibility of librarians and libraries. What is the culpability of those library staff members who were directly involved in the decade long process? It was they who discriminated against their colleagues, they who identified materials for removal and organised their removal and destruction and they who changed catalogue records. Can they claim the Nuremberg defence, that they were 'just following orders'? What about those who were aware of the process of cultural cleansing but stood by silently? Most of us were ignorant of those actions, should we have cultivated greater watchfulness? How can we ensure that such a pattern of events will never happen again?'

Source: Byrne, A. (2002) 'Introduction', in *The Ethics of Librarianship: An International Survey*, München: K.G. Saur, p. 11.

Anti-USA Patriot Act militancy

Federal Bureau of Investigation (FBI) agents are 'particularly frustrated that they cannot get approval to use Section 215 of the Patriot Act, called the 'library provision' by Patriot Act critics because it could be used to search library or any other business records. One FBI e-mail from 2003 complains that the Office of Intelligence Policy and Review (OIPR) 'should be embarrassed that the FBI has used this valuable tool to fight terrorism exactly ZERO times'. The e-mail goes on: 'The inability of FBI investigators to use this seemingly effective tool has had a direct and clearly adverse impact on our terrorism cases. While radical militant librarians kick us around, true terrorists benefit from OIPR's failure to let us use the tools given to us.'

Source: *http://www.npr.org/templates/story/story.php?storyId=5049679* (accessed 8 November 2006).

Mobilisation

Definition

The process by which individuals or sections of society become active and organised towards social change. In sociology and politics: the process by which a passive collection of individuals in a society is transformed into an active group in the pursuit of common goals, or coerced into political participation by an authoritarian government. (OED)

Example

Librarians' role in the publishing of Michael Moore's Stupid White Men

A Buzzflash interview with Michael Moore dated March 13, 2002 points to the important role that librarians who mobilized in the cause of intellectual freedom played in the publication of his best-selling book, *Stupid White Men*:

'*Buzzflash*: Now specifically, a little bit about your book. You've written in your columns that after September 11th, your publisher was going to deep-six the book unless you took out critical comments on Bush. You held firm. Is it true that the librarians of America came to your defense and saved the day?

Michael Moore: That's what it looks like. I mean, I didn't know who any of these people were. They – this one librarian found out about it and she got in a, I don't know, library chat room. Or she sent a letter out to a list of librarians and they sent it out to a bunch of people and the thing kind of mushroomed from there. So, I'd say it's a combination of these librarians and the Internet, because they started sending letters to Harper-Collins and Harper-Collins saw that it wasn't gonna be a good thing to ban the book. But I'm really happy about it. I really didn't realize the librarians were, you know, such a dangerous group.

Buzzflash: Subversive.

Michael Moore: They are subversive. You think they're just sitting there at the desk, all quiet and everything. They're like plotting the revolution, man. I wouldn't mess with them. You know, they've had their budgets cut. They're paid nothing. Books are falling apart. The libraries are just like the ass end of everything, right?'

Source: *http://www.buzzflash.com/interviews/2002/03/Michael_Moore_031302.html* (accessed 8 November 2006).

Movement

Definition

A change of place or position; a progress, change, development, etc. (OED)

Example

Critical library movement

The *critical library movement* is, perhaps, the best example of how *movement* is manifest in library and information work for social change. This author's description of critical library movement provides historical context. The critical library movement (which incorporates, at least, progressive librarianship, socially responsible librarianship, activist librarianship, radical librarianship, independent librarianship, alternative librarianship and anarchist librarianship) 'has a tradition that dates from the late 1930s in the US when library activists of the 1930s pressured the ALA to be more responsive to issues put forth by young members involved in such issues as peace, segregation, library unions and intellectual freedom. By 1940, a new group called the Progressive Librarians' Council emerged in order to provide a united voice for librarians who sought change in the association. By the end of its first year, the Progressive Librarians' Council had 235 members. Many were involved with ALA's Staff Organizations Round Table, formed in 1936 and Library Unions Round Table, formed in 1940. In addition, the Progressive Librarians' Council Bulletin provided a forum for activities on behalf of freedom of expression. The Bulletin printed outspoken opinions "not tolerated" by the traditional communication organs – Library Journal, Wilson Library Bulletin and ALA Bulletin. [Thus since, the critical library movement has produced its own vehicles of discourse with a network base in such places as Africa, Argentina, Austria, Canada, Germany, Mexico, Sweden, the UK and the USA]. This discourse gained significant momentum in the late 1960s/early 1970s in the USA and elsewhere in the 1980s. In the last decade, the decentralized and multidirectional technology and communications infrastructure of the Internet has greatly enhanced relationship building, grassroots democratic organizing and the development of 'new citizenship groups' around the discourse and practice of critical librarianship.'

Source: Samek, T. (2004). 'Internet and intention: an infrastructure for progressive librarianship', *International Journal of Information Ethics* 2(11): 2–5. [In summer 2005, the online journal name changed to *International Review of Information Ethics.*]

Nonviolent direct action

Definition

Non-violent direct action is any form of direct action that does not rely on violent tactics. (Wikipedia)

Historical example

Librarians' participation in a peaceful protest of the Vietnam war

In the context of ALA history, '1967 was a watershed year, in large part because librarians who introduced the concept of social responsibility in behind-the–scenes discussions, turned their talk into action. At the annual ALA conference in San Francisco, a group of librarians publicly protested during a pro-Vietnam war speech by General Maxwell D. Taylor. Although protesting librarians represented only a tiny fraction of peace activists, the fact that some took a public stand on a so-called non-library issue was significant.' This event was the first of a series of catalysts that introduced a professional identity crisis in US librarianship during the period 1967–74. The crux of the crisis was highly charged debate about the concept of library neutrality. It was during this period that the Social Responsibilities Round Table of the ALA was formed.

Source: Samek, T. (2001) *Intellectual Freedom and Social Responsibility in American Librarianship, 1967–1974.* Jefferson, NC: McFarland & Company, Inc.

Contemporary example

Martyn Lowe papers

Martyn Lowe is the founder of Librarians Within the Peace Movement. His papers, housed in the International Institute of Social History in Amsterdam, include letters and other documents regarding issues of censorship, freedom and ethics in various countries, sent to 'Information for Social Change' 1993–1998; documents regarding 'Librarians within the Peace Movement' 1991–1993; documents regarding the Library and Information Workers Organisation (LIWO) in South Africa and the issuing of its newsletter 'Liwolet' 1991–1999; documents on the Ecomemoria Project, part of the Human Rights International Project, London, an organisation that works against human rights violations and to put an end to impunity in Chile 2001–2002; and stationery of the War Resisters' International.

Source: *http://www.iisg.nl/archives/en/files/l/10886415.php* (accessed 8 November 2006).

Organisation

Definition

The action or process of organising, ordering, or putting into systematic form; the arrangement and coordination of parts into a systematic whole; *spec.* the action of banding together or gathering support for a political cause. (OED)

Example

Librarians Without Borders

Librarians Without Borders (LWB) was founded in February, 2005 at the Faculty of Media and Information Studies at the University of Western Ontario in London, Ontario, Canada. 'LWB is composed of Master of Library and Information Science students and LIS professionals from across Canada and the United States. The group is already 200 members strong and growing! LWB strives to improve access to information resources regardless of language, religion, or geography, by forming partnerships with community organizations in developing regions. We envision a global society where all people have equal access to information resources.'

Source: *http://www.lwb-online.org/* (accessed 8 November 2006).

Refuge

Definition

Shelter or protection from danger or trouble; succour sought by, or rendered to, a person. (OED)

Example

Libraries as places of refuge

According to Nancy Kranich, 'The tide of the twenty-first century carried Americans into ever-deeper engagement in the life of their communities. The terrorist attacks on September 11, 2001 sharply accelerated that movement. "There is a new spirit here and it's one of warmth, solidarity, humanity and determination that we have not witnessed before", Justice Sandra Day O'Connor observed during a visit to New York City.

Libraries in New York and around the country provided comfort, fellowship, news and resources during this difficult period. School, public and academic libraries stayed open to provide shelter for displaced and lonely residents needing help and the solace of others. Internet and phone banks were set up to connect with family and friends and to view news updates. Library web sites linked citizens to disaster and recovery information, charitable organizations and helpful resources to calm children and adults alike.'

Source: Kranich, N. (2001) 'Libraries create social capital'. Available from: *http://www.libraryjournal.com/article/CA180511.html* (accessed 1 July 2006).

Resistance

Definition

The act, on the part of persons, of resisting, opposing, or withstanding. (OED)

Example

Resolution 5, on Cuba, passed at the 58th Annual General Meeting of the Canadian Library Association

'*Whereas* Cuba is a small impoverished island country of 11 million people; and *Whereas* Cuba has achieved for its entire population a high standard of healthcare, basic literacy, nutrition and education; and *Whereas* Cuba has been subject to continuous foreign attempts to undermine its government through economic blockades, subversion, military adventures, assassination attempts and funding of political opposition through "civil society" organizations; and *Whereas* Cuba is being challenged by foreign governments and organizations for not upholding the core library principles of intellectual freedom and access to information regarding its libraries as part of a broader effort to overthrow the Cuban government; and *Whereas* ending such foreign intervention is a precondition for enabling Cuba to develop fully its own social economy and broad democratic participation and debate; and *Whereas* Cuban libraries can play an important role in developing a full and democratic culture within Cuba; *Resolved that* CLA oppose any foreign government attempts to undermine Cuba's government through economic blockades, subversion, military adventures, assassination attempts and outside funding of political opposition through "civil society" organizations; and *Be it further resolved that* CLA call upon the International Federation of Library Associations and Institutions (IFLA) to convene an international commission of eminent librarians to hold public hearings to investigate further the role of "independent libraries" in Cuba and charges that they are funded through foreign agencies whose political program is regime change; and *Be it further resolved that* CLA encourage such a Commission to publish and disseminate widely the results of its findings. MOVED: Brian Campbell. SECONDED: Martin Dowding. CARRIED.'

Source: Canadian Library Association (2003) Resolution 5, on Cuba, passed at the 58th Annual General Meeting of the Canadian Library Association in Toronto, Ontario, 23 June. Available at: *http://www .cla.ca/resources/resolutions2003.htm* (accessed 8 November 2006).

Revitalisation

Definitions

Revitalisation: The action of revitalising, or the fact of being revitalised. (OED)

Revitalise: *trans*. To restore to vitality; to put new life into. (OED)

Example

Libraries are not for burning: International librarianship and the recovery of the destroyed heritage of Bosnia and Herzegovina

András Riedlmayer's paper, presented at the 61st IFLA General Conference in 1995, is a contemporary example of an international effort to revitalise libraries and other cultural institutions in a former war zone. In the abstract to his paper, he writes that 'In the past three years, the cultural heritage of Bosnia-Herzegovina has suffered major destruction. The result is what a Council of Europe report has called "a cultural catastrophe". Historic architecture (including 1,200 mosques, 150 churches, 4 synagogues and over 1,000 other monuments of culture), works of art, as well as cultural institutions (including major museums, libraries, archives and manuscript collections) have been systematically targeted and destroyed. The losses include not only the works of art, but also crucial documentation that might aid in their reconstruction. Our Bosnian colleagues need the assistance of the international library community to help them recover and reconstruct some of what has been lost and to rebuild the buildings and institutions that embody their country's cultural heritage. The paper suggests some innovative ways that librarians outside of Bosnia, through their home institutions and professional organizations, can provide material and technical assistance, training and documentation to help to undo the destruction of memory.'

Source: Riedlmayer, A. (1995) 'Libraries are not for burning: International librarianship and the recovery of the destroyed heritage of Bosnia and Herzegovina'. Available at: *http://www.ifla.org/IV/ifla61/61-riea.htm* (accessed 8 November 2006).

Solidarity

Definition

The fact or quality, on the part of communities, etc., of being perfectly united or at one in some respect, esp. in interests, sympathies, or aspirations; *spec.* with reference to the aspirations or actions of trade-union members. (OED)

Example

Cuban Libraries Solidarity Group

At the Third International Congress of Culture and Development, held in Havana in 2003, the Cuban Library Support Group was relaunched as the Cuban Libraries Solidarity Group (CLSG). 'The organization was established on July 1, 1999 to support: Cuban libraries, librarians, library and information workers and the Cuban Library Association (ASCUBI); Cuba's [cost] free and comprehensive education system and high literacy levels; the Cuban people's right to self-determination and to choose the social, political and economic systems which support their library service.'

Source: *http://www.cubanlibrariessolidaritygroup.org.uk/* (accessed 8 November 2006).

Struggle

Definition

An act of struggling; a resolute contest, whether physical or otherwise; a continued effort to resist force or free oneself from constraint; a strong effort under difficulties. (OED)

Example

Progressive African Library & Information Activists' Group and the struggle for democracy

The Progressive African Library & Information Activists' Group consists of a group of progressive African librarians and information workers who 'recognise that current "leaders" in the African information field have done little to break the colonial and imperialist policies and practices in meeting the information needs of working people in Africa, or to make the profession more relevant to the needs of African librarians and information workers. We have therefore decided to take the initiative to set up an alternative organisation – the Progressive African Library and Information Activists' Group. PALIAct will provide a new vision to help create a people-orientated information service that can meet the information needs of workers and peasants. It will work towards providing an anti-imperialist and a Pan-African world outlook among African librarians and information workers. It will also seek to set up an alternative information service in partnership with the potential users of the service as a way of showing what our "official" libraries and information workers should be doing. PALIAct will form partnerships with progressive information and other workers within Africa and overseas. The Project will bring together the resources, skills and labour of those who accept its vision for a relevant information service, based on the principles of equality, equity, social justice and democracy.'

Source: *http://www.pambazuka.org/index.php?id=28705* (accessed 8 November 2006).

Survival

Definition

Continuance after the end or cessation of something else, or after some event; continuance of a custom, observance, etc. after the circumstances or conditions in which it originated or which gave significance to it have passed away. (OED)

Example

Advocacy for library services to address poverty, homelessness and people living on fixed income, such as the ALA's Hunger, Homelessness and Poverty Task Force

The report 'Are public libraries criminalizing poor people?' challenges policy makers and front-line librarians to review the ALA's Policy 61 ('Library Services for Poor People') and ask themselves the following questions: 'Do I understand the scope of poverty in my community and its human face? Are our programs and services inclusive of all poor people and their needs? Do we actively partner with social service providers and anti-poverty groups? Do we advocate for public funding of programs that help poor people? Do our actions address core problems or simply treat superficial symptoms?'

Source: ALA (2005) 'Are public libraries criminalizing poor people?: A report from the ALA's Hunger, Homelessness and Poverty Task Force', *Public Libraries* 44(3): 175 .

Note

1. Welton, N. and Wolf, L.; photography by Wolf, L. (2001) *Global Uprising: Confronting the Tyrannies of the 21st Century: Stories from a New Generation of Activists*, Gabriola Island, BC: New Society Publishers.

5

Specific forms of social action used in library and information work for social change

This section showcases creative social action strategies used by library and information workers worldwide. The strategies represent library and information workers' political and transformative acts of resistance to ideological domination in the present realities of war, revolution, social change and global market fundamentalism. Some of the strategies documented involve varying degrees of personal and professional risk, depending on the political, legal, economic, technological, ideological and cultural contexts of the countries and communities in which library and information workers live and labour, as well as more personal factors such as the gender, class, nationality, ethnicity, sexual orientation and race of library and information workers themselves. Many of the strategies recognised are practised in the international critical library community, where considerations for the human condition and for human rights take precedence over other professional concerns.

As with the previous section, effort has been taken to provide clear and practical examples of each action item on the list. However, particularly with this list, examples are not exhaustive or mutually exclusive; indeed, examples overlap. For example, 'Letters' overlaps with 'Petitions', and 'Awards' overlaps with 'Scholarships'. Readers are therefore reminded to modify and develop the examples in consideration of the contexts within which they live and labour. The examples that comprise the alphabetical list are presented in Table 4.1.

Unless otherwise noted, definitions of the strategies are derived from the following online resources:

Table 1 Social action strategies used by library and information workers worldwide

Access to information	Law reform
Accessibility	Letters
Action research	Listservs
Activism, honouring of	Lobbying, government
AIDS information and awareness	Manifestos
Alternative action programmes	Media relations, management of
Apologies	Meeting room policies
Awards	Meetings with government
Bibliographies	Memory projects
Blogs and blogging	Merchandise
Book fairs	Mobile libraries
Books	Music
Borrowing	Naming, responsible
Boycotts	Outreach activities
Campaigns	Pandemics, response to
Classification schemes	Partnerships
Collection development and collection development policies	Petitions
	Platforms
Collections	Position statements
Community development	Posters
Community studies	Proclamations
Conference guides and sessions	Programmes
Cooperation, international	Programmes for children and youth
Cooperation, multidisciplinary	Projects
Court cases	Protests
Critical dialogue	Public forums
Cultural diversity training	Publications
Declarations	Rallies
Dedications	Reaffirmations
Disaster response	Representation
Dissent	Resolutions
Diversity action programmes	Resource sharing
Documentation	Round tables
Eco-friendliness	Scholarships
Education, LIS	School libraries, alternative
Election guides/kits	Security, humane
Ethics training	Seminars
Expositions	Space, autonomous
Film	Speeches
Forums	Storefronts
Fundraising	Student engagement
Historicism	Symposiums
Intellectual freedom	Teaching
Interest groups	Training, activist
International development	Translations
Interviews	Trustees, education of
Investing, socially responsible	Websites
Job postings	Wikis
Labelling	Women, status of

- Online Dictionary for Library and Information Science (ODLIS): *http://lu.com/odlis/index.cfm*
- Oxford English Dictionary Online (OED): *http://www.oed.com/*
- Wikipedia – The Free Encyclopedia: *http://en.wikipedia.org/*

Sources of direct quotations are given at the end of each entry in the 'Source' section.

Access to information

Definition

The right of entry to a library or its collections. All public libraries and most academic libraries in the USA (and in select other countries) are open to the general public, but access to certain areas such as closed stacks, rare books and special collections may be restricted. In a more general sense, the right or opportunity to use a resource that may not be openly and freely available to everyone. (ODLIS)

Examples

E-LIS

'*E-LIS* is an open access archive for scientific or technical documents, published or unpublished, on Librarianship, Information Science and Technology and related areas. E-LIS relies on the voluntary work of individuals from a wide range of backgrounds and is non-commercial. It is not a funded project of an organization. It is community-owned and community-driven. We serve LIS researchers by facilitating their self-archiving, ensuring the long-term preservation of their documents and by providing word-wide easy access to their papers.'

Source: *http://eprints.rclis.org/* (accessed 8 November 2006).

Blue Trunk libraries

'The Blue Trunk library is a collection of one hundred or so books on medicine and public health, together with three or four subscriptions to medical journals. The collection, which is organized according to major subjects, has been developed by the Library of the World Health Organization for installation in district health centres as a means of compensating for the lack of up-to-date medical and health information. In order to make it easier to transport and store, the collection has been packed into a blue metal trunk fitted with two shelves on which the cardboard boxes containing the books are arranged.

The Blue Trunk libraries project starts in a country with the approval of the Ministry of Health, which appoints a national project coordinator. It is with the Coordinator that the WHO librarians establish a dialogue, with the cooperation of the Office of the WHO Representative. The Coordinator acts as an adviser, passing on observations and experience. The Coordinator follows up and supports the project by visiting districts to organize workshops on medical and health information. If necessary, he/she serves as a link between the districts and the country's medical libraries to provide additional information to health professionals. The Coordinator assesses the project's relevance and success by gathering statistics and through regular discussions with the BTL assistants. In order to establish a genuine network and a dialogue among the sites, a Blue Trunk libraries bulletin (which may be no more than an information sheet) will be published in each country to gather and report the experiences of the project's partners. An intercountry edition of the bulletin will regroup all the experience and provide information on the project's progress in the different countries.'

Source: Certain, E. (1998) 'Blue Trunk libraries', *WHO Liasons* 9: 2–6. Available from: *http://www.who.int/library/country/liaison/1998/liaison_9-3_eng.pdf* (accessed 2 July 2006).

Accessibility

Definition

The ease with which a person may enter a library, gain access to its online systems, use its resources and obtain needed information regardless of format. In a more general sense, the quality of being able to be located and used by a person. In the Web environment, the quality of being usable by everyone regardless of disability. See the Web Accessibility Initiative. (ODLIS)

Example

Access to Libraries for Persons with Disabilities: Checklist

'This checklist – developed by the IFLA Standing Committee of Libraries Serving Disadvantaged Persons (LSDP) – is designed as a practical tool for all types of libraries (public, academic, school, special) to (1) assess existing levels of accessibility to buildings, services, materials and programs and to (2) enhance accessibility where needed.'

Source: Irvall, B. and Nielsen, G. S. (2005) *Access to Libraries for Persons with Disabilities: Checklist,* The Hague: International Federation of Library Associations and Institutions.

Action research

Definition

Research that each of us can do in our own practice, that 'we' (any team or family or informal community of practice) can do to improve its practice, or that larger organisations or institutions can conduct by themselves, assisted or guided by professional researchers, with the aim of improving their strategies, practices and knowledge of the environments within which they practise. (Wikipedia)

Examples

Curry, A. (2005) 'Action research in action: Involving students and professionals', Proceedings of the World Library and Information Congress, 71st IFLA General Conference and Council. Available at: *http://www.ifla.org/IV/ifla71/papers/046e-Curry.pdf* (accessed 2 July 2006).

Farmer, L. S. J. (2003) *How to Conduct Action Research: A Guide for Library Media Specialists*, Chicago, IL: American Association of School Librarians.

Activism, honouring of

Definition

Activism: A doctrine or policy of advocating energetic action. Hence activist (æktvst), an advocate of activism in either sense. (OED)

Activism, in a general sense, can be described as intentional action to bring about social or political change. This action is in support of, or opposition to, one side of an often controversial argument. The word 'activism' is often used synonymously with protest or dissent, but activism can stem from any number of political orientations and take a wide range of forms, from writing letters to newspapers or politicians, political campaigning, economic activism (such as boycotts or preferentially patronising preferred businesses), rallies and street marches, strikes, or even guerrilla tactics. In the more confrontational cases, an activist may be called a freedom fighter by some and a terrorist by others, depending on whether the commentator supports the activist's ends. (Wikipedia)

Example

Getting Libraries the Credit they Deserve: A Festschrift in Honor of Marvin H. Scilken

'*Maverick Librarian Marvin Scilken Dies at ALA Midwinter.* Indefatigible librarian and library advocate Marvin H. Scilken, who was serving his 20th year as an ALA Council member, died of an apparent heart attack early on the morning of February 3 in Philadelphia. At the time of his death, Scilken, 72, was attending ALA's 1999 Midwinter Meeting. Founder and editor of *The U*N*A*B*A*S*H*E*D L*I*B*R*A*R*I*A*N*, Scilken was director of the Orange (NJ) Public Library from 1964 until his retirement in 1993, a 1992–93 petition candidate for the ALA presidency and a frequent contributor to the *New York Times'* letters to the editor. His 1966 testimony before the US Senate Subcommittee on Anti-Trust and Monopoly on alleged price fixing of library books triggered more than 1,000 lawsuits and individual libraries' recovery of millions of dollars. Three decades later, Scilken spearheaded a successful campaign to stop Bell Atlantic from charging libraries for other phone companies' directories. At a memorial during the February 3 Council session, ALA President Ann Symons called Scilken 'our conscience', adding that 'he never hesitated to puncture our complacency.'

Source: Roy, L. and Cherian, A. (eds) (2002) *Getting Libraries the Credit they Deserve: A Festschrift in Honor of Marvin H. Scilken*. Lanham, MD: Scarecrow Press. See: *http://lists.webjunction.org/wjlists/publib/ 1999-February/087701.html* (accessed 8 November 2006).

Affirmative action programmes

See Diversity action programmes

AIDS information and awareness

Definition

Acquired Immune Deficiency Syndrome (AIDS): an illness (often if not always fatal) in which opportunistic infections or malignant tumours develop as a result of a severe loss of cellular immunity, which is itself caused by earlier infection with a retrovirus, HIV, transmitted in sexual fluids and blood. (OED)

Example

How information managers and librarians can make a difference

'The author develops the view that as long as information managers, librarians and libraries guard, keep and hold on to information, there will never be peace. Women issues are still a 'taboo' in many cultures in Africa and librarians and information managers seem to embrace the condition in a surprising professional complicity. Yet women issues are *all the people's* issues. As information managers become immune to information development on issues that concern women, they help deduct from world peace. Women issues especially in Africa need to be addressed seriously, whether on rape of young children especially the girl child, female genital mutilation, the recruitment of boy soldiers, poverty, *the HIV/ AIDS scourge that has destroyed the family*, environment degradation, or education for women. The author also examines whether there are formally trained information managers in Kenya who can address the issues' (Abstract, emphasis added).

Source: Wagacha, W. P. (2005) 'How information managers and librarians can make a difference'. Available at: *http://www.ifla.org/ IV/ifla71/papers/162e-Wagacha.pdf* (accessed 27 June 2006).

Alternative action programmes

Definitions

Programme: A definite plan or scheme of any intended proceedings; an outline or abstract of something to be done (whether in writing or not). Also a planned series of activities or events. (OED)

Alternative: Of two things: Such that one or the other may be chosen, the choice of either involving the rejection of the other (sometimes of more than two). (OED)

Example

First Social Forum on Information, Documentation and Libraries: alternative action programs from Latin America for the information society

An alternative to IFLA's 2004 conference in Buenos Aires: 'The *First Social Forum on Information, Documentation and Libraries: alternative action programs from Latin America for the information society*, held in Buenos Aires from August 26–28, 2004, was called by the Social Studies Group on Library Science and Documentation (Argentina) and the Study Circle on Political and Social Librarianship (Mexico).' It resulted in the Declaration from Buenos Aires on Information, Documentation and Libraries, which is in wide international circulation and available now in (at least) the following languages: Spanish, English and German.

Source: *https://arl.org/Lists/SPARC-OAForum/Message/1352.html* (accessed 8 November 2006).

Apologies

Definition

Justification, explanation, or excuse, of an incident or course of action. (OED)

Example

Greater Victoria (British Columbia) Public Library Board's apology to fired employee John Marshall

'In 1954, the Greater Victoria Public Library Board fired one of its employees, John Marshall, because of his alleged left-wing political affiliations. Although he denied being a Communist, the mayor of Victoria threatened to burn subversive library books and the chief librarian resigned over the controversy. Almost a half-century later, in November 1998, the Board presented a public apology to John Marshall for its mistreatment of him. It also announced that the British Columbia Library Association would name its intellectual freedom award in his honour.'

Source: *http://www.ifla.org/faife/report/canada.htm* (accessed 8 November 2006).

Awards

See also Scholarships

Definition

Something conferred as a reward for merit; a prize, reward, honour. (OED)

Examples

Miriam Braverman Memorial award

'The Miriam Braverman Memorial Prize is awarded annually for the best essay written by a student of library/information science on an aspect of the social responsibilities of librarians, libraries or librarianship. The prize is named in honor of Miriam Braverman (1920–2002), an activist librarian who was a longstanding member of the Progressive Librarians Guild and a founder of the American Library Association's Social Responsibilities Round Table. She was a strong proponent of the social responsibilities perspective within librarianship and an inspiration to younger librarians entering the field.'

Source: *http://libr.org/plg/2006_BravermanAward.html* (accessed 8 November 2006).

Progressive Librarians Guild opposes 'award' to Laura Bush

'On April 10, 2005, the American Library Association launched National Library Week, during an event at the Martin Luther King Jr. Public Library in Washington DC, by publicly recognizing Mrs Laura Bush's activities on behalf of libraries. PLG voices opposition to this recognition on the following grounds: (1) The American Library Association is actively opposed to sections of the USA Patriot Act. Mrs Bush has publicly stated her complete support for the USA Patriot Act ... (2) Since the public is highly unlikely to know that this recognition was given in the absence of any discussion by ALA's governing body and is also largely unlikely to separate the Mrs Bush who supports the USA Patriot Act from the Mrs Bush who supports libraries, the public perception created is that ALA endorses Mrs Bush period. (3) The granting of awards within ALA is conducted according to clearly delineated processes.'

Source: Progressive Librarians Guild (2005) 'Progressive Librarians Guild opposes "award" to Laura Bush'. Available at: *www.libr.org/plg/LauraNo.html* (accessed 27 October, 2006).

Bibliographies

Definition

A list of the books of a particular author, printer, or country, or of those dealing with any particular theme; the literature of a subject. (OED)

Example

Bibliography on library services to poor people

In 2002, this online bibliography was compiled by Ariel Collins as part of a directed study on library services to poor people at the School of Library and Information Studies, University of Alberta. This bibliography targets the public library sector.

Source: Ariel W. Collins (2002) 'Bibliography on library services to poor people'. Available at: *http://www.slis.ualberta.ca/cap03/ariel/home.html* (accessed 27 October 2006).

Blogs and blogging

Definitions

Blog: A frequently updated website consisting of personal observations, excerpts from other sources, etc., typically run by a single person and usually with hyperlinks to other sites; an online journal or diary. (OED)

Blogging: The activity of writing or maintaining a weblog. (OED)

Example

The log of a librarian

'We are the managers of world's memory, a memory made of paper, ink and plastic, a labile memory which needs organizers. This is not a forum, but the diary of an Argentinian Librarian, where a professional (but primarily a human being) will express his search of an identity and a dream, living in a painful reality. Some ideas are here... I invite all of you to share them with me.'

Source: Civallero, E. 'The log of a librarian'. Available at: *http://thelogofalibrarian.blogspot.com/* (accessed 27 October 2006).

Bookmobiles

See Mobile libraries

Book fairs

Definition

A trade exhibition, usually held annually, at which book publishers and distributors display their products in spaces called *booths* leased for that purpose. Also refers to a non-trade exhibition of books and the book arts open to the general public, which may include presentations by authors, illustrators, publishers, binders, etc. (ODLIS)

Example

Support for book fairs by Information for Social Change

Information for Social Change organises 'seminars and conferences, sometimes in association with other progressive organisations such as LINK and the Black Radical and Third World Book Fair. The Better Read than Dead conferences, for example looked at non-capitalist library provisions in Cuba, Vietnam, North Korea and China. The conference proceedings were subsequently published.'

Source: *http://www.libr.org/ISC/who.html* (accessed 8 November 2006).

Books

Definition

A collection of leaves of paper, parchment, vellum, cloth or other material (written, printed, or blank) fastened together along one edge, with or without a protective case or cover. The origin of the word is uncertain. It may be derived from the Anglo- Saxon *boc* (plural *bec*) or from the Norse *bok*, meaning 'book' or 'beech tree', possibly in reference to the wooden boards originally used in binding. Also refers to a literary work or one of its volumes. Compare with monograph. (ODLIS)

Example

Globalisation, Information and Libraries: The Implications of the World Trade Organization's GATS and TRIPS Agreements

'Though it has the subtitle "The implications of the World Trade Organization's GATS and TRIPS agreements", it would have been necessary to write such a book even if GATS and TRIPS had never existed. Or, to put it in the author's own words: *"Therefore, if the GATS does not materialise for whatever reason, then it is highly likely that some other similar agreement would take its place, with an agenda for the liberalisation of trade in services"* ... The words that Ruth Rikowski uses are, to sum up: "Global Capitalism in the Age of the Knowledge Revolution". That gives a hint as to the scope of this book. It goes from the concrete experiences of the library floor through to the dream of a life beyond capitalism.'

Source: Review of Rikowski, R. (2005) *Globalisation, Information and Libraries: The Implications of the World Trade Organization's GATS and TRIPS Agreements,* Oxford: Chandos. Available at: *http://www.foreningenbis.org/Word/LasseReview.doc* (accessed 8 November 2006).

Borrowing

Definition

The action of the verb *borrow*; taking on loan, taking at second-hand, etc.; also that which is borrowed. (OED)

Example

A Malmö library programme allowing patrons to 'borrow' a member of a minority group, in an effort to foster social tolerance

'A Swedish library, realizing that books are not the only things being judged by their covers, will give visitors a different opportunity this weekend – to borrow a Muslim, a lesbian, or a Dane.

The city library in Malmö, Sweden's third-largest city, will let curious visitors check out living people for a 45-minute chat in a project meant to tear down prejudices about different religions, nationalities, or professions. The project, called Living Library, was introduced at Denmark's Roskilde Festival in 2000, librarian Catharina Noren said. It has since been tried at a Copenhagen library as well as in Norway, Portugal and Hungary.

The people available to be 'borrowed' also include a journalist, a gypsy, a blind man and an animal rights activist. They will be available Saturday and Sunday in conjunction with a Malmö city festival and are meant to give people "a new perspective on life", the library said in a statement. "There are prejudices about everything", Noren said. "This is about fighting those prejudices and promoting coexistence".'

Source: *http://www.advocate.com/news_detail_ektid19850.asp* (accessed 8 November 2006).

Boycotts

Definition

To combine in refusing to hold relations of any kind, social or commercial, public or private, with (a neighbour), on account of political or other differences, so as to punish him for the position he has taken up, or coerce him into abandoning it. (OED)

Example

San Francisco Marriott Hotel vs. American Library Association

'The ALA chose to use the San Francisco Marriott (4th St.) as its headquarters hotel during their June 2001 annual conference at the Moscone Center. This hotel has been the site of the largest and longest running labor dispute in the city and is the subject of an ongoing boycott. In 1996 a majority of Marriott employees voted to be represented by the Hotel Employees and Restaurant Employees Union Local 2. After four years of unsuccessful negotiations with the hotel, the union called for a boycott of the San Francisco Marriott Hotel. Despite requests from various ALA members, the union, the San Francisco Library Commission, San Francisco City Librarian and San Francisco Board of Supervisors, ALA refused to make alternative arrangements for meetings, events and lodging scheduled for the San Francisco 4th Street Marriott ... Union members, librarians and other supporters have scheduled a series of protests in front of the hotel during the ALA conference: "Close the book on the Marriott".'

Source: *http://www.holtlaborlibrary.org/boycott.html* (accessed 8 November 2006).

Campaigns

Definition

(a) Applied to any course of action analogous to a military campaign, either in having a distinct period of activity, or in being of the nature of a struggle, or of an organised attempt aiming at a definite result. *(b)* Esp. in politics, an organised course of action designed to arouse public opinion throughout the country for or against some political object, or to influence the voting at an election of members of the legislature. (OED)

Example

Rebuilding of Baghdad Library Campaign

'The National Mobilization Committee for the Defense of Iraq (NMCDI) in Jordan has initiated an academic book collection campaign for Iraq. The goal of this campaign, which has been dubbed "the rebuilding of the Baghdad Library", is to provide Iraqi students, academics and intellectuals with scientific and academic books and references that have been prohibited entry to Iraq for the past ten years. The excuse used is that these items are considered to be "double usage items". Thus Iraqis have been denied the right to learn which is an internationally recognized and protected right...

Politics aside, we simply believe that it is immoral to deny 22 million Iraqis the gift of knowledge. Iraq's historical legacy is that it is the cradle of civilization and it gave humanity the first form of script and the first legal doctrines. In our time, Iraq was able was able to offer free education from kindergarten through university. However, after the destruction of the Iraqi economy as a result of the sanctions and the severe UN restrictions imposed on Iraq, its legacy and achievements have been reduced to day-to-day survival...

Our major goal is to collect and forward to Iraq the 8,000 academic and scientific references needed by Iraqi universities and academic institutions, in an effort to replenish their empty libraries.

Therefore, our committee is contacting as many institutions, organizations and individuals as possible to participate in our campaign.'

Source: *http://www.freearabvoice.org/iraqBookCampaign.htm* (accessed 8 November 2006).

Classification schemes

Definition

A list of classes arranged according to a set of pre-established principles for the purpose of organising items in a collection, or entries in an index, bibliography, or catalogue, into groups based on their similarities and differences, to facilitate access and retrieval. In the USA, most library collections are classified by subject. Classification systems can be enumerative or hierarchical, broad or close. In the USA, most public libraries use Dewey Decimal Classification, but academic and research libraries prefer Library of Congress Classification. (ODLIS)

Examples

Sanford Berman's tireless efforts to improve cataloguing policy, especially the Library of Congress Subject Headings

'Sanford Berman, former head cataloger at Hennepin County Library (HCL) and long-time activist, is well known in the library world for his valiant and unrelenting efforts to reform cataloging and classification practice. In his position at HCL, Berman proactively worked to improve the catalog by applying subject headings that would be more accessible to the patrons, but were not authorized by the Library of Congress.

Berman's quest to rid the LCSH of bias and inequities began when he was working as an assistant librarian at the University of Zambia where colleagues at the library informed him that using 'kafirs', an approved subject heading in LCSH, was akin to calling an American a 'nigger' (Gilyard, 1999). Ever since, Berman has worked to make the LCSH more inclusive of underrepresented and minority groups and less "...Eurocentric, Christian-oriented, male dominated [and] establishment pimping..." (Gilyard, 1999). If Berman and his staff at HCL felt that the subject headings approved by LCSH were either inaccessible or inappropriate, they would create new ones and make recommendations to the Library of Congress for changes to the authority lists. Under Berman, the HCL subject headings were distributed widely by way of the *HCL Cataloging Bulletin*.'

Source: *http://www.slais.ubc.ca/courses/libr517/02-03-wt2/projects/berman/biography.htm* (accessed 8 November 2006).

HURIDOCS

In 1981, Martin Ennals, former Secretary-General of Amnesty International and founding president of Human Rights Information and Documentation Systems, International (HURIDOCS), observed despite a standardised, universal and statutory concern for human rights, that there is no universal and homogenous system of handling information about human rights. This dearth of information standards, techniques and appropriate technology for human rights violations information classification, documentation, reporting and storage led Ennals and others in the global human rights community to propose a Human Rights International Documentation System, leading to the formal establishment of HURIDOCS in 1982. HURIDOCS Offices are located near Geneva, Switzerland.

Source: Human Rights Information and Documentation Systems, International. Available at: *http://www.huridocs.org/about.htm* (accessed 27 October 2006).

Collection development and collection development policies

See also Collections

Definition

A formal written statement of the principles guiding a library's selection of materials, including the criteria used in making selection and deselection decisions (fields covered, degrees of specialisation, levels of difficulty, languages, formats, balance, etc.) and policies concerning gifts and exchanges. An unambiguously worded collection development policy can be very helpful in responding to challenges from pressure groups. (ODLIS)

Examples

Collection Building by the Seat of Your Pants

This website is maintained by Chris Dodge, former public librarian, who urges collection developers to 'Keep your eyes open. Pick up printed matter wherever you go: community centers, co-ops, record stores, coffee shops, laundromats, doctors' offices, the sidewalk. Glean information from these about *other* unfamiliar publications. Send for sample copies of things that sound interesting. Don't be afraid to occasionally read things with smeary ink, sharp staples, small print and clumsy design. Attend zine shows, comics conventions, book fairs and the like. Ask friends who travel to send you their finds.'

Source: *http://www.geocities.com/SoHo/Cafe/7423/collectionbuilding .html* (accessed 8 November 2006).

Collections

See also Collection development and collection development policies

Definition

The total accumulation of books and other materials owned by a library, catalogued and arranged for ease of access, often consisting of several smaller collections (reference, circulating books, serials, government documents, rare books, special collections, etc.) (ODLIS)

Example

Biblioteca Popular José Ingenieros, Buenos Aires, Argentina

The Biblioteca Popular (Ramíres de Velasco 958 (1414), Buenos Aires, *www.nodo50.org/bpji*) 'holds arguably the second largest archival collection of anarchist material in South America. This collection represents a dedication to the preservation of anarchist history, popular education and radical opposition. The library staff accept donations of books and other publications.'

Source: World Infoshops and Zine Libraries. Available at: *http://www .undergroundpress.org/infoshops-world.html* (accessed 8 November 2006).

Community development

Definition

A broad term applied to the practices and academic disciplines of civic leaders, activists, involved citizens and professionals to improve various aspects of local communities. Community development seeks to empower individuals and groups of people by providing these groups with the skills they need to effect change in their own communities. These skills are often concentrated around building political power through the formation of large social groups working for a common agenda. Community developers must understand both how to work with individuals and how to affect communities' positions within the context of larger social institutions. (Wikipedia)

Example

Working Together: Library-Community Connections

'In 2004, Vancouver Public Library initiated a project to develop methods for libraries to work with low-income communities through a community development approach and to explore ways to overcome systemic barriers to library use by the socially excluded.

Funded by Human Resources Development Canada, the Libraries in Marginalized Communities project included Halifax Public Libraries, Toronto Public Library and Regina Public Library. Community Development Librarians (CDLs) would work in the community and with the community, to determine how best the library could serve its needs. After only a few months of community work, the CDLs argued the project title did not fit either the project's goals or the reality of their work. The title was changed to Working Together: Library–Community Connections. In that title change lays the essential difference between the outreach work normally associated with libraries and the concept of community development.'

Source: Campbell, B. (2005) '"In" versus "with" the community: Using a community approach to public library services', *Feliciter* 6: 271–3.

Community studies

Definition

A demographic study of the community served by a library or library system, or of its registered users or user group, for the purpose of measuring economic, social and educational variables pertinent to the development of collections, services and programmes and to the design of new facilities. A profile is usually conducted with the aid of a survey instrument but may also include data compiled from other sources. (ODLIS)

Example

Making a difference in the lives of prostitutes in the midst of a Muslim Sharia State: a voyage of discovery by a female librarian in Northern Nigeria

'This study is a personal attempt by a local librarian to find out how libraries in Kano could make the first attempt to collect, analyse and present a report on the needs of these women in terms of education, health and economics (things they will need to get empowered) and then to report the findings to the government and non-governmental organizations in Kano for appropriate action to solve the problems and change the lives of the prostitutes of Gada village, Nigeria.'

Source: Badawi, G. (2005) 'Making a difference in the lives of prostitutes in the midst of a Muslim Sharia State: a voyage of discovery by a female librarian in Northern Nigeria'. Available at: *http://www.ifla.org/ IV/ifla71/papers/198e-Badawi.pdf* (accessed 7 July 2006).

Conference guides and sessions

Definition

Conference: A formal meeting of a group of individuals, or representatives of several bodies, for the purpose of discussing topics and/or making decisions on issues of mutual interest, for example, the

Charleston Conference, an annual meeting of librarians, publishers and vendors. When published collectively, any papers presented at such a meeting are known as proceedings. (ODLIS)

Examples

ALA Annual Conference Disorientation Guide, Washington DC, 1998

Sessions and activities described in the alternative guide to the 1998 ALA conference included: Must the Poor Always Be Among Us?; What Have You Done for Me Lately?: Lesbian and Gay Youth Speak Out; Anarchist Librarians Beer Night; Free Speech Buffet; and Street Libraries: Infoshops and Alternative Reading Rooms. The latter was given the following description: 'Anarchist and punk information workers? Partly a response to public libraries' failure to meet the real needs and desires of young people and activist communities, a network of alternative libraries and infoshops has grown during the 90s in North America. Learn more about these spaces being staked out for use as zine archives, meeting rooms, day care centers, concert venues, free skools and bookstores, from the folks who run them.' Sponsored by: ALA Social Responsibilities Round Table, Alternatives in Print Task Force; Task Force on Hunger, Homelessness and Poverty; Progressive Librarians Guild; ALCTS Collection Management Discussion Group; Association of College and Research Libraries (ACRL); Women's Studies Section; and Young Adult Libraries Services Association (YALSA).

'Beyond ALA', a Counterpoise post-conference, Orlando, 2004

'The Counterpoise Advisory Board and the Counterpoise Collective are organizing a small post-conference immediately following ALA's 2004 Annual Conference in Orlando. Librarians, publishers and users are invited to discuss aspects of library service that are under or over-emphasized, misrepresented, or ignored by mainstream libraries and library organizations. There is no consensus about a framework for the conference. Some participants may take ALA as a benchmark, considering areas that it avoids or insufficiently addresses. Others may posit the opposite of ALA – global instead of national vision, library workers and users instead of institutions, democracy instead of administrative hierarchies. Others may ignore ALA altogether and develop independent approaches to issues of acquiring, organizing, storing and disseminating information and knowledge for use. The conference will be relaxed and informal, with panel discussions and individual presentations that encourage audience participation.'

Source: *http://www.librarianactivist.org/news/counterpoise.html* (accessed 10 July 2006).

Cooperation, international

Definition

Library contacts with members of similar groups in other countries. (Akribie – Arbeitskreis kritischer BibliothekarInnen [Working Group of Critical Librarians, Germany]).

Example

Lib-plic

Lib-plic is an active contemporary international library network of progressive librarians who participate in 'exchanging views, submitting early warnings, sending signed petitions or other letters on urgent issues' that threaten libraries and intellectual freedom. Lib-plic organises 'in common with other cultural and educational progressives, to help put issues of social responsibility on the agendas of international bodies such as IFLA and UNESCO.'

Source: *http://www.foreningenbis.org/English/lib_plic.html* (accessed 10 July 2006).

Cooperation, multidisciplinary

See also Partnerships

Definition

Cooperation: The action of cooperating, i.e. of working together towards the same end, purpose, or effect; joint operation. (OED)

Multidisciplinary: Combining or involving several separate academic disciplines. (OED)

Example

African Information Ethics Symposium: Ethical Challenges in the Information Age

The first ever Africa Information Ethics Symposium was held in Pretoria in February, 2007. The South African government, in close collaboration with NEPAD, invited a number of African participants with multidisciplinary focus on information policy implications. Topics included cultural diversity and globalisation; development, poverty and ICT including information poverty; global security, human security; spamming and other forms of information wrongdoings; information corruption and information injustice; protection and promotion of indigenous knowledge; respect for human dignity – information rights; freedom of expression; freedom of access to information (IP legislation, open access movement, TRIPS); privacy and the role of Ubuntu; North-South flow of information and information imperialism; Internet and exclusion (socio-political and economic exclusion); foundations of African information ethics; using ICT for a better life in Africa: case studies; E-Government; and related topics. The main focus was to understand and reflect on these issues in the light of their ethical context within the African context and possible policy implications. International invitees represented Africa, South Africa, Europe, Asia, Southeast Asia, North America, and Latin America and the Caribbean.

Source: *http://www.africainfoethics.org/* (accessed 7 January 2007).

Court cases

Definition

Law. A cause or suit brought into court for decision. (OED)

Example

US Circuit Court of Appeals for the District of Columbia ruling against 'broadcast flag' copy protection

In May 2005, the US Circuit Court of Appeals for the District of Columbia issued a decisive 3-0 opinion in favour of libraries and consumers when it ruled that the FCC overstepped its jurisdiction by mandating a 'broadcast flag' copy protection in new technologies. 'The decision is being hailed as a significant step towards restoring the rights of consumers to make lawful copies of digital content. "This is a big victory for consumers and libraries", said Emily Sheketoff, executive director of the American Library Association (ALA) Washington Office, representing the petitioners in the case. "The broadcast flag seriously undermined the rights allowed nonprofit educational institutions under the TEACH Act to distribute digital content over the Internet for distance learning purposes. It even imposed restrictions on how consumers are able to use digital content in their own homes ... The FCC order required that all digital electronic devices, such as television sets and personal computers, include code that accompanies digital television (DTV) signals to prevent redistribution of the digital content over the Internet".'

Source: *http://www.ala.org/ala/washoff/washnews/2005ab/050may06 .htm* (accessed 8 November 2006).

Critical dialogue

Definition

Dialogue encouraging thought about the usual or prescribed practice, reflecting on the practical work undertaken in libraries (Akribie – Arbeitskreis kritischer BibliothekarInnen [Working Group of Critical Librarians, Germany]).

Example

Progressive Librarians Guild

The Progressive Librarians Guild is committed to 'providing a forum for the open exchange of radical views on library issues; to conducting campaigns to support progressive and democratic library activities locally, nationally and internationally; to supporting activist librarians as they work to effect changes in their own libraries and communities; to bridging the artificial and destructive gaps between school, public, academic and special libraries and between public and technical services; to encouraging debate about prevailing management strategies adopted directly from the business world, to propose democratic forms of library administration and to foster unity between librarians and other library workers; to critically considering the impact of technological change in the library workplace on the provision of library services and on the character of public discourse; to monitoring the professional ethics of librarianship from a perspective of social responsibility; [and] to facilitating contacts between progressive librarians and other professional and scholarly groups dealing with communications and all the political, social, economic and cultural trends which impact upon it worldwide, in a global context.'

Source: *http://www.libr.org/plg/* (accessed 10 July 2006).

Cultural diversity training

Definition

Cultural diversity and human rights: Culture takes diverse forms across time and space. This diversity is embodied in the uniqueness and plurality of the identities of the groups and societies making up humankind. As a source of exchange, innovation and creativity, cultural diversity is as necessary for humankind as biodiversity is for nature. In this sense, it is the common heritage of humanity and should be recognised and affirmed for the benefit of present and future generations (UNESCO Declaration on Cultural Diversity, Article 1).

Example

The role of the Cultural Awareness Officer in the Rotherham Metropolitan Borough Council, UK

'Cultural Awareness Officer: Serving the needs of minority ethnic communities is a key element in providing a fully inclusive library service. The Cultural Awareness Officer working closely with and reporting to the Manager, Social Inclusion and Project Development ensures that this is comprehensively addressed and fully covered in the Social Inclusion Action Plan. This officer trains and raises awareness amongst staff, contributes to the selection and presentation of library materials and advises on signing, guiding and promotion. The officer liaises with representatives of all the minority ethnic communities in Rotherham. He will be accredited under the Quality Leaders Project for Black Library and Information Workers (QLP). The QLP addresses policy areas around exclusion and the provision of public services to minority ethnic communities.'

Source: Rotherham Metropolitan Borough Council (2004) 'Library and information services social inclusion policy'. Available from: *http://www.rotherham.gov.uk/graphics/Learning/Libraries/Services+Off ered+by+Your+Library/_Inclusionservices.htm* (accessed 8 November 2006).

Declarations

Definition

The action of stating, telling, setting forth, or announcing openly, explicitly or formally; positive statement or assertion; an assertion, announcement or proclamation in emphatic, solemn, or legal terms. A proclamation or public statement as embodied in a document, instrument or public act. (OED)

Example

The Kampala Declaration on Intellectual Freedom and Social Responsibility (1990)

'*Preamble*: Intellectual freedom in Africa is currently threatened to an unprecedented degree. The historically produced and persistent economic, political and social crisis of our continent continues to undermine development in all spheres. The imposition of unpopular structural adjustment programmes has been accompanied by increased political repression, widespread poverty and intense human suffering. African people are responding to these intolerable conditions by intensifying their struggles for democracy and human rights. The struggle for intellectual freedom is an integral part of the struggle of our people for human rights. Just as the struggle of the African people for democracy is being generalised, so too is the struggle of African intellectuals for intellectual freedom intensifying. *Aware* that the African states are parties to international and regional human rights instruments including the African Charter on Human and People's Rights and *convinced* that we, the participants in the Symposium on "Academic Freedom and Social Responsibility of Intellectuals" and members of the African intellectual community, have an obligation both to fight for our rights as well as contribute to the rights struggle of our people, we met in Kampala, Uganda, to set norms and standards to guide the exercise of intellectual freedom and remind ourselves of our social responsibility as intellectuals. We have thus adopted the Kampala Declaration on Intellectual Freedom and Social Responsibility on this 29th day of November, 1990. May the Declaration be a standard-bearer for the African intellectual community to assert its autonomy and undertake its responsibility to the people of our continent.'

Source: *http://www1.umn.edu/humanrts/africa/KAMDOK.htm* (accessed 10 July 2006).

Dedications

Definition

A note prefixed to a literary, artistic or musical composition dedicating it to someone in token of affection or esteem. (*American Heritage Dictionary*)

Example

A special issue of SLIC Online dedicated to the firebombing of the United Talmud Torah Grade School in Montreal

'This special issue of SLIC Online was conceived in response to the firebombing of the United Talmud Torah grade school library in Montreal, Quebec in the early morning hours of April 5, 2004. Founded in 1876, the United Talmud Torah is Canada's oldest Jewish day school and a Canadian institution. The destruction of its grade school library is a new threat to the tradition of intellectual freedom and cultural democracy in Canada. From the umbrella organization, the International Federation of Library Associations and Institutions (IFLA), down to national, provincial/state and local associations around the world, library rhetoric and policy on intellectual freedom recognizes the inherent relationship between human rights and freedom of expression. This powerful connection is embedded in Article 19 of the United Nations Declaration of Human Rights ... I hope that people from around the world examine this issue of SLIC Online and use it to strengthen their understanding of the role that librarians play in the human rights agenda, including freedom of expression, cultural democracy and the rights of the child.'

Source: Samek, T. (2004) 'So we never forget the destruction of United Talmud Torah grade school library' *SLIC Online* 23(4). Available at: *http://www.schoollibraries.ca/articles/39.aspx* (accessed 22 October 2006).

Demonstrations

See Rallies *and* Protests

Dialogue

See Critical dialogue

Disaster response

Definition

Activities that occur in the aftermath of a disaster to assist victims and to rehabilitate or reconstruct the physical structures of the community. (UN Office for the Coordination of Humanitarian Affairs, *http://www.irinnews.org/webspecials/DR/Definitions.asp* (accessed 8 November 2006))

Example

Geaux Library Recovery: Information Community Disaster Assistance Network

'*Geaux Library Recovery* is dedicated to bringing Information Professionals from around the country together to offer volunteer help to our Gulf Coast colleagues and friends impacted personally and professionally by Hurricane Katrina. We're here to lend a helping hand in any way we can.' The first call for help sought out those 'dedicated to assisting with library and archive recovery and clean-up and to help information professionals and their families recover from the most catastrophic natural disaster in American history. "Restoring and guaranteeing the safety and well-being of all people in the affected areas should be the Number One priority of all American relief efforts", Jason Jackson, a visiting librarian at Miami (OH) University and Geaux Team Member, said. Once the proper disaster recovery agencies have made the situation stable enough for recovery of some of the nation's most valuable treasures and important libraries to commence, Geaux Library

Recovery volunteers will be ready. The Gulf region of the United States is home to some of the world's oldest and most important historical collections, including the Greater New Orleans Collection, The William Ransom Hogan Archive of New Orleans Jazz, the Archive of New Orleans and the New Orleans Museum of Art. Additionally, the region is served by numerous public libraries and historical societies, many of which were underfunded and understaffed before Hurricane Katrina. "We're calling on all institutions, large and small, to coordinate local recovery support efforts, to conduct community outreach and educational responses, as well as to provide as much support of local disaster charity organizations as humanly possible. We want to send a message to the world that we will not let the Gulf region's information centers, their collections, or their staff and patrons, down", Jackson added. "It is the ethical and moral responsibility of archivists, conservation and preservation experts, librarians, Information Technologies professionals and historians to make sure our friends and colleagues have the support they need, when they need it most." The Geaux Library Recovery effort is working towards developing strategic partnerships with other professional organizations, including the American Library Association, the Louisiana Library Association, the Northeast Document Conservation Center, SOLINET, the Society of Southwestern Archivists, the Society of American Archivists, the National Park Service and various other agencies to help meet possible supply and volunteer labor needs. Volunteers will be ready and waiting to offer any support to these organizations in their efforts to help the Deep South recover from Katrina's aftermath. Geaux Library Recovery is actively soliciting only trained professionals in the area of collection disaster recovery, all aspects of librarianship, systems support, historic preservation, repository construction and renovation, archival management and administration and conservation of historical sites, collections and properties.'

Source: *http://geauxlibraryrecovery.blogspot.com/* (accessed 8 November 2006).

Dissent

See also Manifestos

Definition

Difference of opinion or sentiment; disagreement; dissension, quarrel. (OED)

Example

Librarians against war: an open letter

Excerpts: 'We speak to you as librarians, members of a humanistic profession whose practice implies commitment to openness, democracy and freedom ... Dedicated to an ideal of human progress which attends to preservation and continuity, librarianship is committed to patient, constructive work for a better future. A profession which helps create and maintain space for discourse and argument, for the free speech and dissent so important to a robust democracy, librarianship is also a profession based on mutuality. This includes international cooperation in the service of a world of knowledge which knows no borders ... As we write, our government is preparing an air assault on Iraq which will be devastating to the already suffering Iraqi people and which will contribute nothing to the cause of democracy or peace. We do not accept the planned death of countless civilians, the destruction of the infrastructure of their lives and society, as an "acceptable price to pay" or as "collateral damage". We speak in solidarity with our colleagues in the nation of Iraq, in its libraries and schools and universities, who strive for freedom and the end of oppression but in no way wish to see their people suffer another round of punitive military attacks and destruction... There are forces, among them the United Nations, which are striving for a diplomatic solution to the impasse over site inspections in the sovereign nation of Iraq. We support all such efforts. With colleagues whose names are signed below, the Action Council of the Social Responsibilities Round Table of the American Library Association voices its opposition to the planned US-led attacks on the nation of Iraq. ... Sincerely, Mark Rosenzweig, SRRT Action Council, Hofstra University – and ...'

Source: Rosenzweig, M. (1998) 'Librarians against war: an open letter', *Progressive Librarian* 14 (spring). Available at: *http://libr.org/pl/14_Letter.html* (accessed 22 October 2006).

Diversity action programmes

Definition

Programme: A definite plan or scheme of any intended proceedings; an outline or abstract of something to be done (whether in writing or not). Also a planned series of activities or events. (OED)

Diversity: Inclusiveness with regard to differences in age, gender, sexual orientation, religious belief and ethnic, racial or cultural background within a given population. (ODLIS)

Example

Seattle Public Library's diversity policy statement

'The Seattle Public Library is committed to providing a workplace environment free of discrimination. The Library shall administer its employment programs so that access, selection and advancement opportunities are made available to applicants and employees based on their relative knowledge, skills and abilities without regard to race, color, sex, marital status, sexual orientation, political ideology, age, creed, veteran's status, religion, ancestry, national origin or the presence of any sensory, physical or mental disability.

This policy supersedes Seattle Public Library Policy #8a: Personnel – Equal Opportunity and Affirmative Action, dated January 17, 1977.'

Source: *http://www.spl.org/default.asp?pageID=about_policies_diversity* (accessed 10 July 2006).

Documentation

The accumulation, classification and dissemination of information; the material so collected. (OED)

Examples

Information for Social Change

'Information for Social Change is an activist organisation that examines issues of censorship, freedom and ethics amongst library and information workers. It is committed to promoting alternatives to the dominant paradigms of library and information work and publishes its own journal, *Information for Social Change*. The ways by which information is controlled and mediated has a serious influence on the ways people think, how they communicate, what they believe is the "real world", what the limits of the permissible are. This applies equally to information that comes through the channels of the mass media, through our bookshops or through our libraries. Of course, free and equal access to information is a myth throughout the world, although different situations pertain in different countries. Control is more explicit and cruder in some places, more "sophisticated" and more invisible elsewhere (for example in Britain). One of the aims of Information for Social Change is to document these situations. But we want to go further than that, documenting also the alternatives to this control, the radical and progressive channels by which truly unfettered, unmediated ideas may circulate. And further still: to encourage information workers to come together, to share ideas, to foster these alternatives – whether we are publishers, librarians, booksellers, communication workers or distributors. Whoever you are, if you are in sympathy with us, join us.'

Source: *http://www.libr.org/isc/who.html* (accessed 10 July 2006).

The lib-plic list

Lib-plic supports 'cooperative collection, organization and preservation of the documents of people's struggles and the making available of alternative materials representing a wide range of progressive viewpoints often excluded as resources from the debates of our times.'

Source: *http://www.foreningenbis.org/English/lib_plic.html* (accessed 10 July 2006).

Eco-friendliness

Definition

Ecologically 'friendly'; not harmful to the environment. Also applied to products manufactured with explicit regard to the environment. (OED)

Examples

Bike rentals for travelling around the annual American Library Association conference, 2005

'For those who wish to travel Chicago by bicycle, discounted rentals are available from Bike Chicago Rentals and Tours, which has three locations:

- Navy Pier – 600 E. Grand Ave. (312) 595-9600
- Millennium Park Bicycle Station – 239 E. Randolph Street (888) BIKE-WAY
- North Ave. Beach – 1600 N. Lakeshore Drive, (773) 327-2706

The discounted rate is $10 per day, which includes the use of a helmet and lock. To receive the discount, just show your ALA Conference badge at the shop.

To reserve your bike please call Bike Chicago (312) 595-9600 or visit *www.bikechicago.com.*

This opportunity is offered only as information to attendees. ALA is in no way connected to the bike company or responsible for the condition or safety of the bikes. This is not an ALA-sponsored activity.'

Source: *http://www.ala.org/ala/eventsandconferencesb/annual/2005a/ generalinfo.htm#bikes* (accessed 8 November 2006).

Donkey libraries in Zimbabwe

'In Zimbabwe, children that have not previously thought of using any kind of technology are now able to use many great electronic devices due to the creation of donkey libraries. Donkeys have provided extensions for libraries, which, as a result, have provided many multi-media services to remote communities throughout Zimbabwe. Some of these services include, radio, telephone, fax, e-mail and the internet. There are currently four donkey drawn libraries being used in the Nkayi district, an area north-west of Zimbabwe. These donkey libraries are very popular and have garnered much international attention.

The donkey mobile units use electro-communication carts, which have solar units on the roof. As a result of these solar units, solar energy charges a battery, which provides the electric power. Furthermore, many electronic materials are used in this cart; for example, in the back of the cart, there are storage cabinets for batteries, inverters, books, music disks, records and videocassettes. Consequently, eighty-six percent of the population in the area served by these donkey libraries can now read.'

Source: *http://www.bookboat.com/unusual_lib/donkey_library.htm* (accessed 10 July 2006).

Education, LIS

Definition

Educational programmes designed to prepare students for the postbaccalaureate degree of MLS or MLIS, taught by the faculty of a university department known as a library school (or school of librarianship). Modern library education began in 1887 when Melvil Dewey founded the first school for training professional librarians at Columbia University. (ODLIS)

Example

A course offered in the Master of Library and Information Studies programme at the School of Library and Information Studies, University of Alberta

'Calendar Description: Examines the central concepts of intellectual freedom and social responsibility and the range of related issues impacting different types of libraries. Course Objectives: Upon successful completion of this course, a student should be able to: (1) analyze, evaluate and articulate the complexities of intellectual freedom and of social responsibility as multi-dimensional and contested concepts; (2) consider interdisciplinary and critical perspectives for examining the library as part of a larger network of cultural production, access, and regulation; (3) analyze how the library and information studies discourse on intellectual freedom and social responsibility interplays with other discourses such as cultural studies, education, philosophy, political science, women's studies, law, communication, publishing, business, information policy, sociology, pedagogy, history, ethnic studies, identity studies, and technology; (4) contextualize the ethos of intellectual freedom and social responsibility in professional discourse in terms of when it emerged, how it evolved and where it is heading; (5) critically evaluate professional issues and core values related to intellectual freedom and social responsibility from various standpoints, e.g. public, school, academic, government, corporate, personal, professional, child, youth, adult, class, race, gender, cultural and literary canons; (6) identify and discuss issues, trends, theories, practices, challenges, concepts, opportunities, threats, history, research and key resources from the standpoint of intellectual freedom and social responsibility in Canadian (and other) libraries; (7) identify and discuss library association rhetoric (e.g. position statements) on and related to intellectual freedom and social responsibility; (8) communicate effectively policy positions on intellectual freedom and social responsibility, through both oral and written means; (9) state key concepts in media response training and media relations management; (10) understand Canadian library and information professionals' roles in promoting and advocating for intellectual freedom and social responsibility.'

Source: *http://www.slis.ualberta.ca/592_outline.htm* (accessed 29 January 2007).

Librarians and Human Rights at the School of Library and Information Science, University of South Florida

'The aim of the seminar, *Librarians and Human Rights,* is to present a historical and cultural analysis of the role of librarians vis-à-vis human rights as defined by the 1948 Universal Declaration of Human Rights. The course will highlight the stated goals of the profession and the work librarians must do to achieve a more equitable society in the United States and a compassionate nation among others.'

Source: *http://www.cas.usf.edu/lis/mccook/librariansandhumanrights .htm* (accessed 8 November 2006).

Election guides/kits

Definitions

Election: The formal choosing of a person for an office, dignity, or position of any kind; usually by the votes of a constituent body. (OED)

Guide: A book of instruction or information for beginners or novices (in an art, etc.) (OED)

Examples

Critical issues facing the Government of Canada

'Chaired by CLA Vice-President Stephen Abram, the Political Action Task Force has been diligently working on key national and regional issues. The result of their deliberations is a 29-page document entitled "Critical issues facing the Government of Canada". This document represents a key tool that can be used by members across the country in ensuring the voice of libraries are heard and to assist members in making these points to their local members of parliament and those who will be seeking election in the various ridings.'

Source: Canadian Library Association (2004) 'Critical issues facing the Government of Canada. Libraries are the answer. Libraries tranform lives", prepared by the CLA Political Action Task Force. *See also: http://www.cla.ca/top/whatsnew/wnap1904_2.htm* (accessed 8 November 2006).

Library Association of Alberta election kit

The Library Association of Alberta election kit was originally produced for the context of provincial Alberta elections. However, the kit helps 'in bringing library issues to the forefront of both the federal and provincial election campaigns'. Select aspects of the kit include how to identify target groups and analyse key communication tools for reaching target groups, defining the message and the instruction that 'just because the election's over don't stop' infusing your message into the political process.

Source: *http://laa.ab.ca/advocacy/advocacy.cfm* (accessed 8 November 2006).

Ethics training

Definition

Ethics: The moral principles by which a person is guided. In a wider sense, the whole field of moral science, including besides Ethics properly so called, the science of law whether civil, political or international. (OED)

Example

Position statement on information ethics in LIS education

The Information Ethics Special Interest Group (IE-SIG) of the Association for Library and Information Science Education (ALISE) formed in April 2005. The rationale for organising was to give critical attention to pluralistic ethical reflection in LIS education. Its charge is to promote the study of information ethics in the LIS curriculum; to support pluralistic dialogue about ethical considerations both within the global LIS community and with partner communities; and to serve as a clearninghouse for teaching, research and service resources in information ethics. With this in mind, over the past year the approximately 75 members of the IE-SIG collaborated on the development of a position statement on information ethics in LIS education (see below for text). To help launch the statement, the IE-SIG sponsored a panel session titled 'An action driven panel/round table discussion on information and professional ethics' on 16 January 2007 at the ALISE conference in Seattle.

'Knowledge and understanding of pluralistic intercultural information ethical theories and concepts, including the ethical conflicts and responsibilities facing library and information professionals around the world, are necessary to relevant teaching, learning, and reflection in the field of library and information studies and information-related professions. Many important areas and issues currently facing library and information professionals can only be understood in light of their ethical contexts. Also, the contributions that library and information studies can make to knowledge societies can be significantly informed by their attention to information ethics.

As suggested by universal core values promoted by the International Federation of Library Associations and Institutions and other professional organizations and world bodies, it is our responsibility to participate critically in the global discourse of information ethics, as it pertains to, at least, the following articles of the Universal Declaration of Human Rights:

- Respect for the dignity of human beings (Art. 1);
- Confidentiality (Art. 1, 2, 3, 6);
- Equality of opportunity (Art. 2, 7);
- Privacy (Art. 3, 12);
- Right to be protected from torture or cruel, inhuman or degrading treatment or punishment (Art. 5);
- Right to own property (Art. 17);
- Right to right to freedom of thought, conscience and religion (Art. 18);
- Right to freedom of opinion and expression (Art. 19);
- Right to peaceful assembly and association (Art. 20);
- Right to economic, social and cultural rights indispensable for dignity and the free development of personality (Art. 22);
- Right to education (Art. 26);
- Right to participate in the cultural life of the community (Art. 27);
- Right to the protection of the moral and material interests concerning any scientific, literary or artistic production (Art. 27).

The Information Ethics Special Interest Group of the Association for Library and Information Science Education strongly advocates that information ethics should be encouraged as an important aspect of education, research, scholarship, service and practice in library and information studies and in other related professions. It therefore advocates that attention to information ethics (either through the curriculum, instructor expertise, resources, or symposia) be developed and enhanced in all programs of library and information studies education. Schools of library and information studies are urged to implement this recommendation to achieve the following desirable outcomes:

1. The curriculum should be informed by information ethics through a unit in the required foundations (or equivalent) course. This unit should cover the following student objectives:
   - to be able to recognize and articulate ethical conflicts in the information field;
   - to inculcate a sense of responsibility with regard to the consequences of individual and collective interactions in the information field;
   - to provide the foundations for intercultural dialogue through the recognition of different kinds of information cultures and values;
   - to provide basic knowledge about ethical theories and concepts and about their relevance to everyday information work; and,
   - to learn to reflect ethically and to think critically and to carry these abilities into their professional life.
2. There should be offered periodically one or more courses devoted specifically to information ethics. Such courses should be taught by a qualified member of the faculty and be based on international literatures from a diversity of viewpoints.
3. Information ethics should be included in study and discussion across the library and information curriculum. It should be infused throughout the curriculum in such areas as management, young adult services, information literacy training and information-technology related courses.
4. There should be ongoing engagement with information ethics, as challenging questions and issues need to be revisited through the lenses of individuals, institutions and societies.

Note: This position statement draws on content produced by the International Center for Information Ethics (ICIE) and on the structure of the Statement on History in Education for Library and Information Science by the Library History Round Table (LHRT) of the American Library Association (ALA).'

Source: Toni Samek, Convenor 2005–2007, Information Ethics Special Interest Group, Association for Library and Information Science Education (ALISE). Available at: *http://icie.zkm.de/publications/virtual Libraries* (accessed 8 November 2006).

Expositions

Definition

The action of putting out to public view; an instance of this; a display, show, exposure. The action or process of setting forth, declaring, or describing, either in speech or writing. (OED)

Example

Biblioteca en Guerra

Paloma Fernández de Avilés (Jefe del Área de Información y Document-ación, Subd. Gral. de Publicaciones, Información y Documentación, Ministerio de Cultura Inaugrual, Madrid, Spain) organised an historical exposition, produced a supporting catalogue and wrote a scholarly address on the timely subject of librarianship in times of war. The exposition opened, to large crowds from the general public, on 15 November 2005 in Madrid, Spain.

Source: *http://www.loquesomos.org/candilejas/arteodesarte/ BIBLIOTECA%20EN%20GUERRA.htm* (accessed 8 November 2006).

Film

Definition

To photograph for use in a cinema or cinematographic device; to exhibit as a cinematographic production; to put on 'the films' or 'the screen'. (OED)

Example

Storm Center (Columbia, 1956)

Director: Daniel Taradash. Screenplay: Elick Moll, Daniel Taradash. Cast: Bette Davis, Kevin Coughlin, Kim Hunter, Brian Keith, Paul Kelly, Kathryn Grant.

'*Storyline*: A powerful tale about Alicia Hull (Davis), a fiery small-town librarian who lives for the change her work gives her to introduce children to the world of books. In return for the funding to build her long desired children's wing, the city council asks her to withdraw the title "The Communist Dream" from the library at the height of the "red scare". When she defies their request, members of the council question some of her past activities and she is fired and branded as a subversive. Judge Ellerbe (Kelly) thinks she has been treated unfairly and calls a town meeting. Paul Duncan (Keith), an ambitious young politician and boyfriend to assistant librarian Martha Lockeridge (Hunter), sees this meeting as an opportunity to make a name for himself where he denounces Hull as a communist. His fiery rhetoric turns the whole town against Hull, except for Freddie (Coughlin), a young boy who had been her special pet. Freddie becomes more and more upset as the town turns against Mrs Hull, until he sets fire to the library. While the library burns, the townspeople have a sudden change of heart and ask her to come back to work and supervise the building of a brand new library.

Library focus: Storm Center is the quintessential anti-censorship film, offering a very strong, positive image of the librarians played by both Davis and Kim Hunter. Even though the storyline is dated and the town's emotional reversal is somewhat unbelievable, Davis is convincing as the principled librarian, especially as she ponders the question "How do you get rid of a book?"'

Source: *http://www.filmlibrarian.info/storm_center.html* (accessed 8 November 2006).

Note: This film is based on some of the real events surrounding American librarian Ruth Brown's dismissal from the public library in Bartlesville, Oklahoma, in 1950. 'Support for the film came from outstanding people like Drew Pearson and Eleanor Roosevelt. ALA's Library Bill of Rights was used in a brochure put out by the Motion Picture Association of America with Eisenhower's Don't Join the Book Burners speech (p.143). ALA's Intellectual Freedom Committee chairman was used as a technical consultant on the script. A pre-release screening of the film was held at the ALA Conference for 2,000 librarians. They were less than enthusiastic about it, for varied reasons. Storm Center received more praise and acceptance abroad. As Robbins sums up, the film was both the Ruth Brown story and the Hollywood story for it captured the reality of the red scare.'

Source: Horn, Z. (2001) 'Book Review: Louise S. Robbins (2000) *The Dismissal of Miss Ruth Brown: Civil Rights, Censorship and the American Library*, University of Oklahoma Press', *Progressive Librarian* 18 (summer).

Forums

See also Symposiums

As the place of public discussion; hence *fig.* (OED).

Examples

Inclusion of library and information workers in World Social Forum activities

In 2006, in Bamako, Mali, library and information workers were, for the first time, secured inclusion in World Social Forum activities. 'Kingsley [Oghojafor, a Nigerian participant] explained the theme of the second part of the Workshop, which was – The role of the libraries in the WSF process. According to him, the WSF process, which includes all the global, regional, national and local social forums since 2001, now needs the involvement of librarians and information professionals more than ever. He introduced the speakers of the second part who will all try to answer the following questions:

- How to raise library-consciousness within the WSF process?
- How to raise WSF-consciousness among the library and information professionals?
- Dissemination of WSF-information via libraries: methods, practical solutions.
- Documentation of the WSF in the public libraries: project strategies, organization and funding.'

Source: *http://www.nigd.org/libraries/libforum/fcForum/view_html? forum_loc=535257049276&topic_id=343484675192* (accessed 10 July 2006).

International Indigenous Librarians Forum

'The Forum is to encourage opportunities to create an on-going interface through which indigenous librarians can continue to share information, contribute to developing solutions to common concerns and affirm the history, knowledge and values of indigenous populations.

This forum will continue to discuss issues discussed in the Third Forum held in Santa Fe, New Mexico in 2003 and look to new issues arising to indigenous librarians the populations they serve.'

The International Indigenous Librarians Forum Vision: 'We, as unified indigenous peoples who work with libraries and information, will ensure the appropriate care, development and management of the indigenous knowledge of generations past, present and future.'

Source: *http://www.nativeculturelinks.com/aila.html* (accessed 8 November 2006).

Fundraising

Definition

Fundraising is the process of soliciting and gathering money by requesting donations from individuals, businesses, charitable foundations or governmental agencies. Although fundraising typically refers to efforts to gather funds for not-for-profit organisations, it is sometimes used to refer to the identification and solicitation of investors or other sources of capital for for-profit enterprises. Fundraising is the primary way that non-profit organisations obtain the money for their operations. (Wikipedia)

Example

Pacific Northwest Library Association Intellectual Freedom Auction

Supporters of the Pacific Northwest Library Association (PNLA) and intellectual freedom have the opportunity to donate items to an annual PNLA Intellectual Freedom auction to benefit future intellectual freedom programmes.

Source: Pacific Northwest Library Association conference programme (2006) 'Common spaces and far out places: libraries in the Pacific Northwest', Valley River Inn, Eugene, Oregon, 9–12 August.

Government lobbying

See Lobbying, government

Government meetings

See Meetings, government

Historicism

See also Memory projects

Definition

A theory, doctrine, or style that emphasises the importance of *history* (*www.m-w.com*).

Example

The library history programme, IFLA conference, Buenos Aires, 2004

'The library history program at the IFLA conference in Buenos Aires (2004) was one of our busiest ever. It included: 1. Joint session between FAIFE and the Library History Section: Experiences of the years of dictatorship and its effect on libraries (attended by 200+ delegates) ... If you are someone who thinks that librarians are harmless, apolitical creatures who mostly concern themselves with organizing books on shelves, then you would have been well advised to have attended this session, which I was privileged to co-chair. The three papers presented at the session revealed how dictatorships in South America in the 1970s and 1980s imposed strict censorship on what libraries – national, university, public – could stock and disseminate. Along with many intellectuals, librarians were persecuted and viciously controlled. Some were imprisoned, or paid with their lives, for defending freedom of expression. The most passionate paper was delivered by the Director of Libraries, Archives and Museums in Chile. As an example of the philistinism of those who tried to destroy intellectual freedom, she related how even books about the Marx Brothers were banned because they were assumed to be associated with the work of the father of communism! Librarians in South America have now emerged from this intellectual "dark age", if anything strengthened by their experience. However, to truly progress they will require greater support from the developed world than they have received in the past'.

Source: Anghelescu H. G. B. (2005) 'Library history at IFLA 2004. The library history section program', *IFLA Newsletter* (April): 3.

Humane security

See Security, humane

Intellectual freedom

Definition

Everyone has the right to freedom of opinion and expression; this right includes freedom to hold opinions without interference and to seek, receive and impart information and ideas through any media and regardless of frontiers. (Article 19 of the United Nations Universal Declaration of Human Rights)

Examples

IFLA/FAIFE's call on the Chinese government to end censorship of the Internet and allow freedom of expression online

'IFLA/FAIFE calls on the Chinese government to end censorship of Internet access and allow freedom of expression online [Media release 13

July 2005]. The International Federation of Library Associations and Institutions (IFLA) Committee on Free Access to Information and Freedom of Expression (IFLA/FAIFE) expresses its deep concern over the state of freedom of access to information on the Internet in China. At a time when China is becoming more and more significant on the world stage in terms of trade and technological development, the increasing curtailment of the freedom of its citizens to access the information they choose is deeply disturbing. In addition to their continuing use of technological restrictions, the Chinese authorities are tightening control of the Internet, through measures against bloggers and website operators. This is an attempt not merely to silence and punish critics of the government, but also to prevent citizens' general interaction in the online public sphere, says the Chair of the IFLA/FAIFE Committee Professor Paul Sturges. IFLA urges rethink: The elimination of freedom of access to information and freedom of expression will deeply affect the development of a country and its people. Those with influence in China must demonstrate their commitment to full participation in the information and knowledge society. This means to actively work for the provision of unrestricted access to information in accordance with Article 19 of the United Nations Universal Declaration of Human Rights. IFLA urges the Chinese government to reconsider their attitudes towards the country's Internet users and permit full freedom expression online. Access to information, knowledge and lifelong learning is central to democratic development and active participation and influence in society. It is a fundamental human right as specified in Article 19 of the Universal Declaration of Human Rights. The Chinese government's attitude towards the circulation of information is one that cannot be reconciled with Article 19 nor the aspirations of the nations attending the World Summit on the Information Society in Tunisia in November 2005. Furthermore, IFLA strongly suggests that western computer companies providing assistance to the government consider the effects of their actions on freedom of expression in the country. China must be seen as more than just a market for western companies to gain a foothold in – it must be seen as a country where citizens have rights to access the information they choose and to disseminate the opinions they hold without consequences.'

Source: *http://www.ifla.org/faife/news/2005/China-Pr-13072005.htm* (accessed 8 November 2006).

IFLA/FAIFE World Report Series

'The *IFLA/FAIFE World Report Series* comprises of two publications, the *IFLA/FAIFE World Report* – published bi-annually – and the *IFLA/FAIFE Theme Report* – published in alternate years. Each year's publication is launched at the annual IFLA World Library and Information Congress. *Theme Report* is thus launched in Buenos Aires in August 2004 and the next *World Report* will be in Oslo, August 2005.

Goal. To offer timely and detailed summaries of the state of intellectual freedom and libraries worldwide, the IFLA/FAIFE Committee has developed the *IFLA/FAIFE World Report Series*. Our ambition is high. We would like the series to become the authoritative source on libraries and information services with regards to intellectual freedom in a global perspective. However, our success in achieving this ambition depends on the availability of the necessary funding for the editorial work and for building a strong research and monitoring unit within FAIFE.'

Source: *http://www.ifla.org/faife/report/intro.htm* (accessed 8 November 2006).

Zero censorship! Who are we kidding?

'Public librarians have long upheld the social justice philosophy of free access to information for all people. The issue of censorship is related to both the professional principles of the Australian Library and Information Association and to the role public librarians have to play in nurturing social capital in our communities. Until now there has been little Australian data on this topic. This paper considers the philosophy of free access to information in the context of contemporary item selection and classification processes within public libraries. The findings of a survey of Queensland public librarians are used to identify current industry attitudes towards the public right to information and to determine the degree to which censorship mechanisms are currently practiced or prevented in public libraries. The findings support those of overseas researchers that stated anti-censorship attitudes are not always indicative of censorship behaviours and that some librarians employ self-censorship with regard to controversial materials in order to avoid censorship challenges. Keywords: Censorship, Intellectual Freedom, Information Suppression, Freedom to Read, Library Acquisitions, Public Libraries, Alternative Literature.'

Source: Moody, K. E. (2004) 'Zero censorship! Who are we kidding? An exploratory analysis of the opinions and experiences of Queensland-based public librarians with regard to the censorship of materials in public library collections', *Australasian Public Libraries and Information Services* 17(4): 168–85. Available at: *http://eprints.rclis .org/archive/00003611/* (accessed 23 October 2006).

Interest groups

Definition

A group of individuals possessing a common identifying interest. (OED)

Example

Libraries in Communities, a Canadian Library Association (CLA) Interest Group

The CLA Libraries and Communities Interest Group (formed in 2006) decribes its terms of reference as follows: 'This interest group focuses on using community development approaches in communities and neighbourhoods to build inclusive and collaborative libraries. Concerned primarily with socially excluded communities and individuals the group focuses on the philosophies, strategies, empathies and self support that librarians need to reduce the rigidity of the relationships between socially excluded communities and the library. The approach is to encourage a dialogue within the interest group to identify and critically evaluate those values and cultures of our libraries that act as systemic barriers to library participation by those who are outside the mainstream of society. Members will challenge the broader library community to reflect on how our fundamental values of inclusiveness have drifted in the pursuit of efficiency and quantification. Members will discuss, promote, and begin to build library services and service models that recognize the needs of our whole communities, regardless of social, economic, political or cultural status. The interest group will provide a supportive and safe environment to those in Canadian libraries who think there is more to library engagement than checklists and programs and who wish to explore ways to broaden and deepen our community connections through collaborative, consultative, and responsive approaches to our communities.'

Source: *http://www.cla.ca/about/igroups/libraries_communities.html* (accessed 8 November 2006).

International development

See also Cooperation, international

Definition

The goal of international development is to alleviate poverty among citizens of developing countries. International development is a multidisciplinary field that may impact poverty reduction, governance, healthcare, education, crisis prevention and recovery and economic restructuring. (Wikipedia)

Examples

Website for Library Practice for Young Learners

'The LPYL project focused on human resource development rather than on the provision of material resources such as computers, books and shelving ... The project was designed to explore some of the untested innovations in the South African Policy Framework among a sample of school librarians in all of South Africa's nine provinces. The project was also designed as a North-South collaboration to provide exchanges of knowledge and expertise between Swedish and South African library personnel. The project has comprised two phases involving South Africa's national and provincial education departments and two South African non-governmental organisations, Sweden's Bibliotek i Samhälle (BiS) and Swedish International Development Cooperation Agency (Sida).'

Source: Library Practice for Young Learners (LPYL) 'School library development in South Africa and Sweden'. Available at: *http://www .foreningenbis.org/lpyl/index.HTM* (accessed 23 October 2006).

International Association of School Librarianship

The first stated objective of the International Association of School librarianship is 'to advocate the development of school libraries throughout all countries'. The Association has an international development special interest group.

Source: *http://www.iasl-slo.org/objectives.html* (accessed 8 November 2006).

Internet sites

See Websites

Interviews

Definition

A meeting of persons face to face, esp. one sought or arranged for the purpose of formal conference on some point. (OED)

Example

Interview with Jenna Freedman on activism, zines and objectivity

QUESTION: 'Why should reference librarians be activists? Isn't our role a neutral one?' ANSWER: 'Why should anyone? Because you want the world to be a better – or how about less cruelly unjust? – place. That was a snap answer and pertains to the librarian as a person. There's so much to say about this! There is no such thing as neutrality, for one. I do try to be neutral at the reference desk, though, if that's your question. I don't wear political pins and I try not to let my bias show. However, I may not appear neutral to everyone. For one thing I've got blue hair. That may cause a patron, depending on what biases inform his or her thinking, to view me as accessible, cool, frivolous, punk, unprofessional, unreliable, or weird. But even if I didn't have an unusual hair color, people would have reactions to me based on my age, gender, race, resemblance to someone they used to know, etc. No one is neutral – on either side of the desk. But I think your question is really more about being an activist at your library/on the job and whether or not that is appropriate. In a way I have the same answer. You're always making a choice. If you only buy books that are positively reviewed in *Choice* or *LJ*, you're being a passivist (I made that word up. What's the opposite of activist?). As an activist librarian and one who wants my library's collection to serve its users – and librarianship – as well as it can, I find alternative sources of reviews and I seek out other avenues, too. For instance I went to a small press book fair this weekend. One of the book fair's organizers was another activist librarian, Karen Gisonny, of NYPL. All I'm trying to get at is that there are ways of being an activist on the job that don't violate attempted neutrality. You can start a zine collection, mount a Gay Pride display in June and one for Civil Liberties in September, or donate your weeded materials to a prison library. Aside from the zine collection, I did all of the above while working at a Catholic college. That's all activism at your library, but there are other ways of trying to achieve change. You can fight the USA Patriot Act by contacting a member of congress, marching in a demonstration, by putting up a sign, refusing to cooperate with the FBI, writing a resolution, or whatever else you can think of. The PATRIOT Act is just one issue; there are plenty of others. The issue that got me fired up enough to work with others to establish *Radical Reference* was the Republican National Convention being held in New York City, a town where the only Republican is our ex-Democrat mayor who bought his election for $50 million. The idea for *Radical Reference* came from wondering how I, especially as a librarian, could express my outrage/effect/change/stand with and in support of the activist community that was going to protest the invasion and the exploitation of 9/11.'

Source: *Tennessee Libraries* (2004) 'Interview: Jenna Freedman. On activism, zines, and objectivity', *Tennessee Libraries* 54(4): 17–25.

Investing, socially responsible

Definition

Often abbreviated to SRI, it is an umbrella term for a philosophy of investing according to both financial and social criteria. SRI investors seek to align their personal values and financial goals by choosing to invest in companies and organisations displaying values comparable to their own. (Wikipedia)

Example

ALA's efforts to build relationships with socially responsible companies

'Background: As discussed at the 2005 Fall Board meeting, the Development Office gathered information on 'socially responsible' investment funds of Domini and TIAA CREF and their criteria for selecting companies for their portfolios. As you may recall, both of these investment firms hold their portfolios to a strict set of social and environmental standards. New companies are added carefully and existing companies are reviewed and upgraded or downgraded based on their performance against the criteria, as well as their overall profitability. We have culled a sampling of 162 corporate prospects from both their investment portfolios to give you a sense of the types of companies we deem to be a good starting point for our cultivation efforts.

Our hope is that the ALA Executive Board will, based on this list of sample prospects and the strict criteria for social responsibility set by Domini and TIAA CREF, approve for the ALA Development Office to use this pool of corporations to gain support for ALA's mission.'

Source: *http://www.ala.org/ala/ourassociation/governanceb/executiveboard/ eboardagenda/midwinter2006a/EBD6_2cover.doc* (accessed 8 November 2006).

Job postings

Definition

Reflects a combination of job description (job duties, qualifications, etc.) information and the terms and conditions of employment associated with the vacancy. (See *http://shr.ucsc.edu/glossary/glossary_shr-home.htm#J* and *http://appointments.uoregon.edu/glossary.htm* – both accessed 8 November 2006).

Example

Job posting for an adult services librarian, Seattle Public Library

'Title: Librarian, Adult Services

Department: Adult Services

Application Deadline: Continuous Recruitment Process – see statement below

Pay Range: $24.42 – $29.62 per hour

Hours: Hours may include Sunday through Saturday and evenings until 8:00 PM.

Overview: The Adult Services Librarian may work at Central Library or branch locations performing all levels of information and reference services, in settings as diverse as our Specialty collections, Quick Information, or at the Reference desk. Successful candidates must have experience or knowledge in collection development with in-depth knowledge as a subject expert in one or more areas. While we value subject matter experts, we also encourage our Librarians to obtain broad general knowledge of materials, authors and resources in a variety of subject areas.

Essential Functions:

- Intellectual Freedom: Support intellectual freedom; assume responsibility for how the Library is perceived by staff and the public; and provide leadership to the Library through collaborative problem solving.

- Public Service: SPL's Librarians provide a full range of services to the public, in person at public service desks, via e-mail and by phone, while ensuring that each individual patron receives the highest possible standard of customer service. One significant aspect of this job is to teach patrons how to use the full range of library technology available to them so they can make effective use of the range of library resources, services and programs that are available. Librarians are also responsible for developing and implementing innovative services and programs for all user groups.

- Outreach: Our Librarians develop and maintain effective relationships with schools, community and business groups, government and civic agencies, current and potential library users and identify and develop other information resources. In addition to representing SPL to a wide range of individuals and organizations to introduce and promote Library services, Librarians help identify emerging community issues and determine the need for related library services, collections and materials. In this way, Librarians ensure that SPL continues to support Seattle's social, educational, cultural and economic systems effectively.

- Resource Development: Librarians ensure that SPL's information resources have depth and scope, reflect new and emerging information needs and effectively serve our highly diverse and growing clientele. They assist with developing and maintaining materials collections and information resources such as print publications, electronic resources and a wide variety of other information media. Librarians also research new information needs and develop creative responses using innovative resources and delivery service methods (for example, electronic resources such as on-line database searching, CD-ROM products and the Internet).

Required Qualifications:

- MLS: To be considered, candidates must have an MLS from an ALA-accredited library school, or Washington State Certification as a Librarian. NOTE: Graduate students in an Accredited MLIS program in their final semester are eligible to apply; however, Washington State Law prohibits an individual from being hired as a librarian unless the MLIS degree has been obtained.

- Intellectual Freedom: Applicants must have a strong commitment to intellectual freedom.

- Training and/or Experience: Candidates must have education, training or experience in providing public service. Depending on the organizational location of a vacancy, specific education, training and/or experience in a unique specialty or service area may also be required.

- Knowledge of Informational Resources: Candidates must have current working knowledge of PCs in a Windows environment and of technological innovations and library applications, especially the ability to use on-line, CD-ROM, Internet and World Wide Web searching methods and information resources. Knowledge of and experience with, DYNIX library automation or a similar system is highly desirable.

- Excellent Customer Service and Communication Skills: The successful candidate will demonstrate a real commitment to public service and possess exceptional interpersonal communication, problem solving, customer relations and teamwork skills. Candidates must be able to communicate clearly, diplomatically and in a friendly and positive manner with library users from diverse ethnic, socioeconomic and cultural backgrounds, as well as with neighborhood-based or special interest groups. Experience in public speaking and formal writing skills are highly desired, as is fluency in a foreign language (particularly Spanish, Asian or Eastern European languages) or American Sign Language. Candidates MUST possess a sense of humor and the ability to demonstrate a positive and enthusiastic commitment to public service.

- Other Required Skills and Abilities: Candidates must be flexible, able to handle multiple competing priorities and tasks, adaptable to change and able to work effectively in a fast-paced, high-volume environment.

Source: *http://www.spl.org/default.asp?pageID=about_jobsvolunteering_jobs_openings_detail&cid=10639083734* (accessed 10 March 2006).

Labelling

Definition

Label: To describe or designate as with a label; to set down in a category. (OED)

Example

Refusal to label expurgated material

'For the past year, 65-year-old Sanford Berman, head cataloger for the Hennepin County library system, has had a problem: Coolio. Among the memos and files stacked on his desk sat a copy of the California rapper's 1995 frat-hop smash, Gangsta's Paradise. Not just any old copy. Call it the "edited" (or "sanitized" or "clean") version. Anyone who's ever pulled one off the shelves at Target knows them all too well. Edited albums are an industry stand-in for the originals – doctored clones in which "offensive material" (as deemed by some retail chains and the Federal Communications Commission) has been smothered by bleeps, dead air and PG-13 language and so come off sounding like Jerry Springer episodes with beats. Late last fall, Berman was instructed by his colleagues in the county library's Popular Materials Collection Group (PMCG) to do his duty: Give the Coolio-lite disc a subject heading that would distinguish it from the 255 other, unadulterated hip-hop CDs the system's 26 primarily suburban branches keep in circulation (including the original Gangsta's Paradise). Berman, however felt this would be "collaborating in censorship" and he refused this work assignment.'

Source: Dolan, J. (1998) 'Bad rap' *City Pages*, 25 November.

Law reform

Definition

The amendment, or altering for the better, of some faulty state of things, esp. of a corrupt or oppressive political institution or practice; the removal of some abuse or wrong. (OED)

Example

ALA's efforts to reform the USA Patriot Act

In a press release, ALA President Michael Gorman said, 'The House of Representatives has joined the Senate in passing a bill that reauthorizes the PATRIOT Act, extending Section 215 of the Act for another four years and adding almost none of the major reforms the library community has striven for since the PATRIOT Act was passed in 2001, hurriedly and without due consideration of Constitutional liberties. The American Library Association has been in the forefront of the battle to reform sections of the PATRIOT Act in order to restore privacy protections to the millions of people who rely on America's libraries. Although most of the moderate, reasonable and Constitutional reforms we sought were not included in the reauthorization bill, our work on restoring privacy and civil liberties to library users is not over. We will continue to argue for a more stringent standard for Section 215 orders, one that requires the FBI to limit its search of library records to individuals who are connected to a terrorist or suspected of a crime. We will also seek the addition of a provision allowing recipients of Section 215 or 505 orders to pose a meaningful challenge to the 'gag' order that prevents them from disclosing the fact that they have received such an order. We are encouraged by Members of Congress' pledges to introduce legislation that will remedy those sections of the PATRIOT Act that infringe on the civil liberties of library patrons and we look forward to working with those Senators and Representatives to repair this deeply flawed legislation.'

Source: *http://www.ala.org/ala/pressreleases2006/march2006/ HousePATRIOTvote.htm* (accessed 8 November 2006).

Letters

Definition

A missive communication in writing, addressed to a person or body of persons; an epistle. Also, in extended use, applied to certain formal documents issued by persons in authority. (OED)

Example

An open letter to the World Intellectual Property Organization written by Zapopan Martín Muela Meza and distributed to the Progressive Library International Coalition listserv

'Dear Colleague: The following open letter will be sent to WIPO, the World Intellectual Property Organization, calling for *transparency*, *participation*, *balance* and *access* in its work. Prior to a large and ambitious publicity campaign, your sign-on to this letter is essential. WIPO is locking NGOs out of its negotiations, using tactics to isolate those governments who stand up for you and hiding the evidence by deleting it from their website. The mentioned letter goes into great detail on this. If you are a computer programmer or politician; if you are ill, if you have an audio/visual or motor impairment, if you are a student, academic, information or knowledge worker, librarian, or citizen concerned about access to information and knowledge and the absence of balance between rightsholders and the public interest within developed countries and mainly in developing/least developed countries, please take a moment to read this and consider signing into it. Things you can do: (1) sign onto the open letter (now available in English and Portuguese) by visiting this link: *http://www .petitiononline.com/wipo/petition.html*, and (2) spread it all over the world by sending e-mails and putting in your webpage a link to the online petition.'

Source: Meza, Z. M. M. (2005) 'Request for endorsement: Open Letter to the United Nation's (UN) World Intellectual Property Organization (WIPO)'. Available at: *http://www.direitorio.fgv.br/cts/blog_commento .asp?blog_id=67&month=10&year=2006&giorno=&archivio=OK* (accessed 8 November 2006)

Listservs

Definition

An electronic mailing list, a type of Internet forum, a special usage of e-mail that allows for widespread distribution of information to many Internet users. It is similar to a traditional mailing list – a list of names and addresses – as might be kept by an organisation for sending publications to its members or customers. (Wikipedia)

Example

PLGNET-L

Progressive Librarians Guild 'has an e-mail discussion list, *PLGNET-L*, for discussing topics of interest and working together. Non-PLG members may subscribe on a read-only basis and can join the discussion if sponsored by a PLG member. Sponsored list participants will be encouraged to join PLG.'

Source: *http://libr.org/plg/elist.html* (accessed 8 November 2006).

Lobbying, government

See also Meetings with government

Definition

To influence (members of a house of legislature) in the exercise of their legislative functions by frequenting the lobby. Also, to procure the passing of (a measure) *through* Congress by means of such influence. To frequent the lobby of a legislative assembly for the purpose of influencing members' votes; to solicit the votes of members. (OED)

Example

The Florida Library Association lobbying the Hillsborough County Commission to reverse a policy preventing libraries from participating in gay pride events

'On June 23, FLA President Nancy Pike sent a letter to the Hillsborough County Commission expressing the deep concern of the Florida Library Association regarding the Commission's decision to adopt a policy requiring Hillsborough Co. government to abstain from participating in gay pride recognition and events and urging it to reconsider the decision. The Commission's action came in response to a display of gay and lesbian literature in a local library. "We are ethically committed to representing multiple points of view and we firmly believe that representing all of the diverse expressions of life in our communities is our responsibility and is protected by the First Amendment," wrote Ms. Pike. "Public libraries are a particularly American institution, intended to ensure an informed electorate and to serve as a forum for the free exchange of ideas that is required in a democracy. The Florida Library Association is committed to continuing that tradition and providing library services to all Floridians." The letter was recommended by the

FLA Intellectual Freedom Committee and endorsed by the FLA Board.'

Source: *http://www.flalib.org/62305letter.html* (accessed 8 November 2006).

Manifestos

See also Dissent

Definition

A public declaration or proclamation, written or spoken; esp. a printed declaration, explanation, or justification of policy issued by a head of state, government, or political party or candidate, or any other individual or body of individuals of public relevance, as a school or movement in the Arts. (OED)

Example

The Friday the 13th Manifesto

'In 1969, a symposium on "Public Library Service to the Black Urban Poor" held at Wayne State University (Detroit, Michigan, USA) issued a document titled the "Friday the 13th Manifesto". It stated "the social crises of the cities have brought people into conflict with the Establishment", that librarianship "reflects the values and attitudes of the Establishment" and that "present" priorities were established in response to the articulated needs of the power structure not unarticulated needs of those outside the power structure. The missive concluded that because "the library profession has been neither neutral nor objective", it must immediately adopt a philosophy of *advocacy* in every respect of its service to the urban poor.'

Source: Correspondence, Clearinghouse, 1969-1070, ALA's Social Responsibility Round Table (SRRT) Papers, Box 7, University of Illinois at Urbana-Champaign, University Archives.

Media relations, management of

Definition

Media relations: The task consisting of building, maintaining and exploiting good relationships with the media. It serves the purpose of enhancing public relations activities. Media relations is relating with communications media in seeking publicity or responding to their interest in an organisation. It is through media relations that public relations specialists are able to establish and maintain communication and relationships between the organisation and print and broadcast media. (Wikipedia)

Management: Organisation, supervision, or direction; the application of skill or care in the manipulation, use, treatment, or control (of a thing or person), or in the conduct of something. (OED)

Examples

Edmonton (Alberta) Public Library's response to calls from community groups to remove revisionist literature from library shelves

In 1988, during the trial of an Alberta schoolteacher accused of denying the Holocaust, the Edmonton Public Library held tightly to the professional value of intellectual freedom while community groups from across Canada called for the removal of revisionist materials from the collection. The Library managed its relationship with the media during the contestation with carefully worded responses to tough, sensitive questions.

Source: Morgan, K. A. (1990) 'Public librarians and revisionist historians'. Non-thesis research project, Faculty of Library and Information Studies, University of Alberta.

The ALA Communication Handbook for Libraries

'This [ALA] handbook was designed to help librarians and others develop and maintain effective relations with the media and win support for libraries and their programs, all with minimal use of precious resources. Starting with the basics, it explains what publicity is and how it can help a library attract attention, create interest and gain support and continues through creating a plan to connect with media.' It addresses print, TV/cable, radio, Internet, wires and newswires. It also covers 'How to create and update your media list', including defining beats and reaching out to ethnic and minority presses.

Source: *http://www.ala.org/ala/pio/mediarelationsa/availablepiomat/ commhandbook.htm* (accessed 8 November 2006).

Meeting room policies

Definition

A written statement of the conditions governing the use of a public meeting room on the premises of a library, including reservation procedures and any restrictions on use. Meeting room policies have been challenged at some public libraries in the USA, particularly over issues of free speech and separation of church and state. (ODLIS)

Example

The Greater Victoria (British Columbia) Public Library Board's resistance to public pressure to refuse meeting space to a right-wing organisation

'The use by an extreme right-wing group of a meeting room at the Greater Victoria Public Library was a volatile and emotionally charged issue in 1998 and 1999. Despite pressure from anti-hate groups, the Library Board reaffirmed its policy of permitting meeting room access to any legally constituted group regardless of political creed and refused to act in place of duly authorized political and police authorities to initiate actions leading to curtailment of basic civil liberties.'

'The Canadian Library Association has unequivocally supported the position of the Library Board and passed a resolution during its annual general meeting in Victoria in June 1998 to endorse the Greater Victoria Public Library's decision to allow any group, even those whose beliefs may be objectionable to society at large, to use their meeting rooms for lawful purposes. At the same time CLA passed a further resolution opposing racism of any kind and affirming the inclusive principles of public library service and access.'

'The issue of an open meeting room policy was also the topic of a general session at the annual conference of the Canadian Library Association in June 2000 in Edmonton, Alberta.'

Source: *http://www.ifla.org/faife/report/canada.htm* (accessed 8 November 2006).

Meetings with government

See also Lobbying, government

Definition

Meeting: The act or an instance of assembling or coming together for social, business, or other purposes; the action of encountering a person or persons. (OED)

Government: The governing power in a state; the body of persons charged with the duty of governing. (OED)

Example

A meeting between ALA President Carol Brey-Casiano and US Attorney General Alberto Gonzales

'In a move designed to try to bridge the gap between the administration's and the American Library Association's (ALA) positions on a contentious section of the USA Patriot Act, ALA president Carol Brey-Casiano met May 2 [2005] with US Attorney General Alberto Gonzales to underscore the significance to the library community of preserving library users' privacy under the act. Gonzales issued the invitation to the meeting in mid-April, according to ALA. Referring to the differences that have split ALA and the administration on the act's Section 215, which allows clandestine law enforcement searches of library records in the name of fighting terrorism, Brey-Casiano says: "I believe we did make progress" toward resolving differences. "[Gonzales] really seemed to be hearing what we had to say", she says. Brey-Casiano added that the two sides still have "a long way to go" to reconcile their differing points of view. The ALA leader emphasized that librarians want to insure that the government does not use the act to monitor the public's reading habits. At the meeting, Gonzales expressed his support for libraries and for continuing a dialogue with the library community"

Source: Weiss, L. (2005) 'ALA chief meets with US Attorney General over Patriot Act', *School Library Journal* (11 May). Available at: *http://www.schoollibraryjournal.com/article/CA600115.html* (accessed 23 October 2006).

Memory projects

See also Historicism

Definition

Memory: The perpetuated knowledge or recollection (*of* something); that which is remembered *of* a person, object or event; (good or bad) posthumous reputation. (OED)

Project: A cooperative enterprise, often with a social or scientific purpose, but also in industry, etc. (OED)

Examples

UNESCO's Memory of the World Programme

The development and sustaining of virtual libraries, archives, depositories and repositories has great potential for collective and cultural memory and the redress of historical inequities. UNESCO's Memory of the World Programme, for example, was created in 1992 in 'an international effort to safeguard endangered documentary heritage of humankind, democratize access, ensure that people become aware of its significance and disseminate widely its derived products.'

Source: Vannini, M. (2004) 'El programa memoria del mundo en America Latina y el Caribe', IFLA World Library and Information Congress, 70th IFLA General Conference and Council, 22–27 August, Buenos Aires.

The Association for the Recovery of Historical Memory, Spain

'After Franco's death in 1975, an official policy of silence about the past became part of a blueprint for Spain's transition to democracy and neither socialist nor conservative governments were inclined to change it. However, many say the silence left a hole in the nation's memory. The nonprofit archives project is the brainchild of a group called the Association for the Recovery of Historical Memory. It uses volunteers, has no government funding and has gathered more than 100 hours of videotaped interviews in the past year and will give them to universities and libraries. "It will be a vaccine against oblivion, says its founder, Emilio Silva".'

Source: Roman, M. (2005) 'Spanish Civil War victims speak out', *Washington Times*, 2 January. Available at *http://www.washtimes.com/world/20050101-113836-3567r.htm* (accessed 7 November 2006).

The Congreso de Lengua, organised by the Spanish and Argentine governments

The Congresso, organised by the Spanish and Argentine governments is designed for the 'recovery and valorization of cultural identities, spirituality and the roots and the memory of native peoples ... necessary to share, recover and strengthen their cultural richness.'

Source: Esquivel, A. P. (2004) 'Between the walls of information and freedom', Keynote Speaker, IFLA World Library and Information Congress, 70th IFLA General Conference and Council Buenos Aires, 22–27 August. Available at: *http://www.ifla.org/IV/ifla70/ps-Perez_Esquivel-e.htm* (accessed 7 November 2006).

Merchandise

Definition

The commodities of commerce; goods to be bought and sold. Branded products used to promote a particular film, pop group, etc., or linked to a particular fictional character. (OED)

Example

Librarians Against Bush merchandise

'Librarians Against Bush is a group of politically active librarians who are concerned about the Bush administration's policies and their effects on civil liberties, privacy, and intellectual freedom. Through legislation such as the USA Patriot Act, a culture of fear has taken root in this country. As librarians, it is our duty to defend the very principles of our profession under the current administration. Librarians and the citizens they serve should be aware of and refuse to live under such policies, even when we are continually told that they are necessities in the fight against terrorism. For, as Benjamin Franklin said, "Any society that would give up a little liberty to gain a little security will deserve neither and lose both".'

The group's merchandise has included such items as buttons, t-shirts, sweatshirts, tote bags, bumper stickers, and coffee mugs. Orders are processed by cafepress.com (*http://www.cafepress.com/buy/librarian/-/pv_design_prod/pg_1/p_storeid.8688529/pNo_8688529/id_3437017/opt_/fpt_/c_360/*).

Source: *http://www.librariansagainstbush.org/mission.html* (accessed 7 November 2006).

Libraries Matter wristbands, lapel pins, etc.

'Libraries matter' is a library awareness campaign sponsored by Alliance Library System, a regional organisation consisting of academic, public, school and special libraries. Illinois is served by nine regional library systems, each providing services to participating libraries in its region. 'Statewide, over 2,500 libraries of all types and sizes are members of library systems. Funding for Illinois Library Systems is provided through the Illinois State Library and the Secretary of State with funds appropriated by the Illinois General Assembly.

Alliance Library System represents a combined client base of nearly one million customers encompassing 268 school, academic, public, medical and corporate member libraries throughout thirty-one counties in western and central Illinois. ALS provides members with resources that place them at the forefront of information technology developments. CARLWeb is our online catalog. It contains four million items and is available to all Illinois citizens.'

Source: *http://www.alliancelibrarysystem.com* (accessed 8 November 2006).

Mobile libraries

Definition

Delivery of library services by physically bringing library staff and materials to the user, for example, in a specially equipped vehicle, such as a bookmobile. Such services may be available to all users, usually on a predetermined schedule, or tailored to meet the needs of a specific category of user (elderly, homebound, developmentally disabled, children in daycare, etc.) (ODLIS)

Examples

A mobile library programme in Thailand, 1986–88

'There were mobile library programs in the refugee camps that were adapted to the needs and life in the camps. They emphasized on promoting the development of young children and love of reading though story telling and puppets. At the same time parents were encouraged to make toys and tell stories to their children. The mobile library also served as moving theatre. Facilitators performed masked plays to attract audience and give the message, then telling folktales, reading books and providing children with puppets and crayons to do art activities. There was a program adapted to Thai children outside the refugee camps near the border. The program was to train volunteers from the villages without a childcare center. The training emphasized storytelling, singing and book reading techniques for young children. They also were trained to assess the development of children using developmental guidelines. The success of this program inspired the writer to work with childcare workers in urban areas and conduct research in slum areas in Bangkok using parental education packages that were comprised of activities and storybooks for decentering egocentrism. Social adjustment of young children whose parents picked up the packages at the playground was higher than those whose parents picked up the packages at the school. These were mobile library programs that inspired love of reading for young children.'

Source: Parkbonngkoch, C. (2000) 'Mobile library program in Thailand border areas', paper presented at the 66th IFLA Council and General Conference, Jerusalem, 13–18 August. Available at: *http://www.ifla .org/IV/ifla66/papers/091-175e.htm* (accessed 23 October 2006).

Argentina's bibliolancha

'Through a special subsidy granted by the CONABIP, the Delta of Parana acquired a boat to offer mobile library services to its population of 7,000 people. These inhabitants live in the islands and margins on the different rivers, streams and channels.

The Bibliolancha is 7.80 meters of length and equipped and adapted like a traveling library. It has 1,500 books, 300 videos and CD-ROMs, a computer, a television, a video cassette player, audio equipment with outside loudspeakers, equipment to measure the depth of the water, VHF radio, an electricity-generating group of 220 volts, cooks and a complementary bath.

Bibliolancha not only provides books to its geographically isolated population, but it also provides access to recreational and cultural resources. This boat is the first of its kind in Argentina.'

Source: *http://www.bookboat.com/unusual_lib/argentina_bookboat.htm* (accessed 23 October 2006).

Music

Definition

Vocal or instrumental sounds put together in melodic, harmonic or rhythmical combination, as by a composer; a composed musical setting (freq. including both melody and accompaniment) to which a poem, etc., may be sung; (also) the musical accompaniment to a ballet, play, etc. (OED)

Example

Musicians and Librarians in Joint Project in Zambia

'Ngenko Kabyema, Director of Zambia's National Library and Cultural Centre for the Blind announced a project with musicians in Zambia to build a facility for recording both music for Zambian musicians and books and material for print-impaired students and recreational readers. Beit Trust in the United Kingdom contributed 30,000 pounds based on Mr Kabyema's proposal for this cooperative venture which accommodates both musicians and blind readers. Recording music is very expensive and the project will provide employment for some blind musicians and instructions for other blind people.'

Source: *http://www.ifla.org/VII/s31/nws1/spring99.htm* (accessed 23 October 2006).

Naming, responsible

Definition

Responsible: Capable of fulfilling an obligation or trust; reliable, trustworthy; of good credit and repute. (OED)

Naming: The action of *name v.* (To call or distinguish by a specified title or descriptive epithet; to describe, recognise, or acknowledge as); an instance or the result of this. (OED)

Example

Edgardo Civallero's efforts to revise the sections of the Universal Decimal Classification system pertaining to South American aboriginal languages and ethnias

Edgardo Civallero, member of the Revision Advisory Comité of Universal Decimal Classification and member of the Standing Committee for Multicultural Populations of IFLA, has made significant efforts to revise and expand the sections of the Universal Decimal Classification system pertaining to South American aboriginal languages and ethnias.

'I have been collaborating with the Universal Decimal Classification Revision Advisory Committee in the elaboraton of a classification scheme of the South American aboriginal languages (and ethnias). These idioms and societies have been neglected and formerly little represented in the tables of UDC (and others, like DDC or LCC). The codes I'm designing will be included (if approved by the Committee) [they were since approved] in Auxiliar Tables 1f ... Maybe you, who read these lines, will think that to write down a classification structure reflecting these languages is a simple matter. Maybe. However, since my first contact with this task, I discovered that nobody knows for certain which indigenous languages are still spoken, who uses them, where they are, how many speakers are there ... Nobody knows if these languages are still spoken ... Nobody knows exactly how they are read, how they interrelate, if they have their own writing systems or not ... These points show by themselves a wide social and historical problem, which maybe does not touch us directly as librarians, but that should touch us as human beings. For such languages (and their speakers and the cultures they represent and codify) are a part of our heritage, of our cultural diversity and of our global identity. But let's forget this initial problem. My "crisis" started when, after sketching "a grosso modo" the classifcatory tree of native languages, I tried to fill the empty squares with names. ... Which reality I must reflect? ... in each one of the Argentinean and South-American indigenous groups. It is not a simple question of words: some of these names reflect a long history of oblivion, scorn, aggression ... By naming a thing or a person, we are setting a personal position in relation to the named thing or person. Thus, we must become conscious of the value of the words we employ; we must think about their meaning and we should be careful in the use of the names of persons and societies ... The Universal Declaration of Linguistic Rights of Barcelona (1996, *http://www.linguistic-declaration.org/index-gb.htm*) points to the necessity of calling the languages according to the names the speakers give to them. A little of ethics push me to avoid the pejorative terms. But the question, my big question, is if a thesaurus or a classification system built with "clean" (but sometimes unknown) terms would be useful for the final users. Maybe it is just a question of trying, for once, if the union of respect + usefulness is possible. Or if, once again, positive values fall under the pressure of suitability...'

Source: Civallero, E. (2006) 'A question of names', The Log of A Librarian (21 June). Available at: *http://thelogofalibrarian.blogspot .com/2005_06_21_thelogofalibrarian_archive.html.* (accessed 10 July 2006). *See also* the works of Sanford Bermand and Hope Olson.

Outreach activities

See also Programmes *and* Programmes for children and youth

Definition

Library programmes and services designed to meet the information needs of users who are unserved or underserved, for example, those who are visually impaired, homebound, institutionalised, not fluent in the national language, illiterate or marginalised in some other way. Large public libraries often have an *outreach librarian* who is responsible for providing such services. (ODLIS)

Example

ProLiteracy Worldwide

'The UN Decade of Literacy (2003–12) presents an opportunity for the global public library movement to reassert its educational and cultural role on behalf of the world's most marginalized population – adult illiterates.'
    'Self-reliance, health, justice, peace, human rights and preservation of the environment are the primary contexts in which ProLiteracy Worldwide attempts to effect social change through literacy training. These common aspirations of the peoples of the world need to be addressed by all of the world's basic institutions including libraries.'

Source: Wedgeworth, R. (2003) 'The literacy challenge', paper presented at World Library and Information Congress, 69th IFLA General Conference and Council, Berlin, 1–9 August. Available at: *http://www.ifla.org/IV/ifla69/papers/118e-Wedgeworth.pdf#search= %22outreach%22* (accessed 23 October 2006).

Pandemics, response to

See also AIDS information and awareness

Definition

Of a disease: epidemic over a very large area; affecting a large proportion of a population. (OED)

Example

Fiction as a tool to fight the HIV/AIDS battle

'HIV/AIDS is cutting a destructive path through the world: UN AIDS statistics paint an alarming picture. Especially hard hit and in grave in danger is the youth of Sub Sahara Africa who do not seem to be getting the warning messages to change attitudes and behaviour. The paper suggests an additional approach using fiction in a dual pronged manner: to teach, warn about dangers of HIV and also teach language skills. It surveys fictional material from different parts of the world, but mostly Southern Africa published anywhere in the world but available to young people in Africa. Fiction material that like the sugar coated pill will do the work in a relatively more user friendly fashion. Several titles published or set in Africa and elsewhere are surveyed and recommendations made.'

Source: Baffour-Awuah, M. (2004) 'Fiction as a tool to fight the HIV/AIDS battle', paper presented at IFLA World Library and Information Congress, 70th IFLA General Conference and Council, Buenos Aires, 22–27 August. Available from: *http://www.ifla.org/ IV/ifla70/papers/082e-Baffour-Awuah.pdf* (accessed 7 July 2006).

Partnerships

See also Cooperation, international *and* Cooperation, multidisciplinary

Definition

The fact or condition of being a partner; association or participation; companionship. (OED)

Example

Canadian Library Association position statement on corporate sponsorship agreements in libraries

The statement says, in part:

'CLA believes that the following principles are important in developing sponsorship policies and agreements. Libraries have a responsibility to:

1. demonstrate that sponsors further the library's mission, goals, objectives and priorities, but do not drive the library's agenda or priorities.
2. safeguard equity of access to library services and not allow sponsorship agreements to give unfair advantage to, or cause discrimination against, sectors of the community.
3. protect the principle of intellectual freedom and not permit sponsors to influence the selection of collections, or staff advice and recommendations about library materials, nor require endorsement of products or services.
4. ensure the confidentiality of user records by not selling or providing access to library records.
5. be sensitive to the local political and social climate and select partners who will enhance the library's image in the community.'

Source: *http://www.cla.ca/about/sponsor.htm* (accessed 10 July 2006).

Petitions

Definiton

More generally: a formal written request or supplication, (now) esp. one signed by many people, appealing to an individual or group in authority (as a sovereign, legislature, administrative body, etc.) for some favour, right, or mercy, or in respect of a particular cause. (OED)

Examples

ALA's Campaign for Reader Privacy

A petition to 'urge representatives in Congress to oppose the re-authorization of Section 215 of the USA Patriot Act (to restore privacy of bookstore and library records).'

Source: *http://www.ala.org/ala/oif/ifissues/issuesrelatedlinks/ patriotactpetition.htm* (accessed 4 December 2006).

Petition re Côte St-Luc municipal library in Montreal

'PEN Canada is an association of writers and supporters formed in 1926 to defend freedom of expression and raise awareness of that right. It is one of 144 centres of International PEN in 102 countries, and uses the power of the word to assist writers around the world persecuted or exiled for the expression of their thoughts.' PEN Canada members were encouraged to sign an online petition protesting the censorship of an exhibition of photographs by the late Zahra Kazemi, which occurred at the Côte St-Luc municipal library in Montreal. The *Against the Censorship of Zahra Khazemi* Petition to Gerald Tremblay, Mayor of Montreal, Robert Libman, Mayor of Côte St. Luc district, and the Côte St. Luc Library was created by PEN Canada (*http://www.pencanada.ca/*) and written by David Cozac.

Petition: 'To: Gerald Tremblay, Mayor of Montreal, Robert Libman, Mayor of Côte St. Luc district and the Côte St. Luc Library. We, the undersigned, join with PEN Canada in calling on the council of the Montreal suburb of Côte-St-Luc to reverse its attempt to restrict freedom of expression and allow the complete exhibit of photos by Canadian Zahra

Kazemi to be displayed in the community's library. Five of 23 photographs by the late photojournalist were removed from a posthumous exhibition at the Côte-St-Luc municipal library after complaints were lodged that they were pro-Palestinian. In response, Kazemi's son, Stéphan Hachemi, said that the collection of photographs, which has appeared in Paris and other cities, should be displayed in its entirety or not at all. Kazemi, who died while in the custody of Iranian security agents in 2003, was killed precisely for her commitment to bear witness to human tragedies, even when powerful forces want no witnesses to their brutality. She brought that commitment to countries across Africa, Latin America, the Caribbean and the Middle East, including Iran and Palestine. As her son said, suppressing such courageous work even after Kazemi's horrific death is "a violation of my mother's spirit". We believe that freedom of expression is at the core of our democracy. When community leaders take the easy way out and respond to complaints by censoring material that some may find controversial, our whole society loses. Instead of the removing pictures someone that someone finds disagreeable, community leaders need to explain how our society is strengthened by allowing debate, discussion and the expression of diverse points of view.

Banning art sets a dangerous precedent, as it only encourages those around the world who wish to restrict freedom of expression. Moreover, libraries must naturally be centres for openness, discussion, debate and controversy. They are the very last places anyone should find censorship. Re-mounting the Kazemis' photo exhibition in its entirety would demonstrate that Canadians are committed to defending the principles of freedom of expression and a genuine diversity of views and opinion here at home. It would be a fitting, if modest, way to pay our respects to a brave woman who was killed because of her commitment to human rights. Sincerely, *The Undersigned.*'

Source: *http://www.petitiononline.com/Khazemi/petition.html* (accessed 8 November 2006).

Platforms

Definition

The ground, foundation, or basis of an action, event, calculation, condition, etc. Now also a position achieved or situation brought about which forms the basis for further achievement. A basis on which people unitedly take their stand and make a public appeal. Also used of public declarations of principles, beliefs, etc., in non-political contexts. (OED)

Example

BiS Platform

BiS is the acronym of the Swedish organisation Bibliotek i Samhälle (Libraries in Society). 'BiS is a socialist organisation open to people working in libraries and to others with an interest in library issues. BiS believes that it is the objective of libraries to defend and further develop democracy: by supporting freedom of speech and helping to guarantee the provision of information as a base for the creation of fully informed public opinion and social criticism; by being a publicly funded and democratically governed institution developed in dialogue with patrons and the community; by reaching out to, promoting literacy amongst and mentoring primarily those who are at risk of being socially excluded from information; by proactively offering information and literature which provides alternative viewpoints and is not easily accessible and serves as an important supplement to popular and widely available commercial sources.'

Source: BiS (1999) 'General platform of BiS'. Available at: *http://www .foreningenbis.org/English/platform.html* (accessed 26 October 2006).

Position statements

Definition

A proposition or thesis laid down or stated; something posited; a statement, assertion, tenet. (OED)

Example

Library History Round Table statement on history in education for library and information science

'Rather than simply train students to be competent, successful practitioners, faculties need to make greater efforts to prepare people who will look beyond their practice and strive continuously to raise the standards of the profession and improve the system in which it functions ... Faculties could do much more to expand the vision of their students by encouraging them to study the history and structure of their profession' (Derek Bok, Higher Learning, 1986).

'A knowledge of history and an understanding of historical methodology are indispensable elements in the education of library and information professionals. A knowledge of history provides a necessary perspective for understanding the principles and practices of information science. Many of the most important issues of our day – including, for example, intellectual freedom, fees for service, service to minorities, access to government information, the role of new technologies and the place of women in the profession – can only be understood in the light of their historical contexts. And the research process, an essential component of contemporary professional education and practice, can be significantly informed by awareness of both historical precedents and historical methodology.

The Library History Round Table of the American Library Association therefore strongly advocates that history and historical methodology be fully incorporated into the curriculum of all programs of library and information science education. Schools of library and information studies are urged to implement this recommendation in the following ways: (1) The entire curriculum should be informed by historical contexts. All courses, regardless of subject matter, should provide a foundation in the historical background of the subject rather than focusing only on current practices and principles. (2) A strong historical component should be part of any required core curriculum. (3) There should be offered, every year, one or more courses devoted specifically to the history of recording, communicating, organizing and preserving knowledge and of the institutions, individuals and professions engaged in such efforts. Such courses should be taught by a qualified member of the faculty and be based on the research literature. (4) Historical methodology and historical approaches to knowledge should be included in the study and discussion of research methods. (5) The use of historical methodology should be encouraged, where appropriate, to investigate issues and problems in library and information science.'

Source: Library History Round Table (1989) 'Statement on history in education for library and information science'. Available at: *http://www.ala.org/Template.cfm?Section=lhrtpositions&Template=/Co ntentManagement/ContentDisplay.cfm&ContentID=20929* (accessed 26 October 2006).

Posters

Definition

A large single sheet of heavy paper or cardboard, usually printed on one side only, with or without illustration, to advertise a product/service or publicise a forthcoming event (meeting, concert, dramatic performance, etc.), intended for display on a bulletin board, kiosk, wall or other suitable surface. (ODLIS)

Example

Vancouver Public Library's non-profit poster/flyer distribution service

Vancouver Public Library's Bulletin Board service includes the invitation to promote non-profit events guided by the library's poster policy. The policy states the Vancouver Public Library 'will distribute posters, flyers, and brochures for non-profit organizations to our branch libraries providing the material is acceptable for posting or distribution ... and providing the event is held in Vancouver or the publication is produced in Vancouver.'

Source: *http://www.vpl.ca/branches/LibrarySquare/bus/services.html; http://www.vpl.ca/general/posterFlyerPolicy.html* (accessed 7 November 2006).

Press releases

See Media relations, management of

Proclamations

Definition

An official announcement, especially one made by a governing authority to the general public. Also refers to the thing proclaimed. (ODLIS)

Example

Proclamation for Banned Books Week

A form available on the ALA website. US librarians are encouraged to adapt it for local use to support the ALA's annual Banned Books Week, celebrating the freedom to read. Excerpt: 'be it further *resolved*, that the _____ Library encourages all libraries and bookstores to acquire and make available materials representative of all the people in our society; and be it further *resolved*, that the _____ Library encourages free people to read freely, now and forever. Adopted by the _____ Library.

Date

City

State'

Source: *http://www.ala.org/ala/oif/bannedbooksweek/bbwlinks/bbwproclamation.htm* (accessed 8 November 2006).

Programmes

See also Outreach activities, Performances, public *and* Programmes for children and youth

Definition

A definite plan or scheme of any intended proceedings; an outline or abstract of something to be done (whether in writing or not). Also a planned series of activities or events. (OED)

Example

The Ten Point Programme for the groups that met at the Vienna Conference of Progressive Librarians, 2000

Selected points: '(1) we shall work towards an international agenda as the basis of common action of librarians everywhere actively committed, as librarians, to social justice, equality, human welfare and the development of cultural democracy ... (7) we will investigate and organize efforts to make the library-as-workplace more democratic and encourage resistance to the managerialism of the present library culture ... (8) we will lead in promoting international solidarity among librarians and cooperation between libraries across borders on the basis of our joint commitment to the Universal Declaration of Human Rights and related covenants which create a democratic framework for constructive cooperative endeavours ... (9) we will organize in common with other cultural and educational progressives, to help put issues of social responsibility on the agendas of international bodies such as IFLA and UNESCO ... (10) we shall oppose corporate globalization which, despite its claims, reinforces existing social, economic, cultural inequalities and insist on a democratic globalism and internationalism which respects and cultivates cultural plurality, which recognizes the sovereignty of peoples, which acknowledges the obligations of society to the individual and communities and which prioritizes human values and needs over profits.'

Source: Rosenzweig, M. (2000) 'Ten point program presented to the groups which met at the Vienna Conference of Progressive Librarians sponsored by KRIBIBIE'. Available at: *http://www.libr.org/PLG/10-point.html* (accessed 26 October 2006).

Programmes for children and youth

See also Outreach activities, Performances, public *and* Programmes

Definition

Programme: A definite plan or scheme of any intended proceedings; an outline or abstract of something to be done (whether in writing or not). Also a planned series of activities or events. (OED)

Youth: Young people (or creatures) collectively; the young. (OED)

Child: A young person of either sex below the age of puberty; a boy or girl. (OED)

Example

Library Services to Youth of Hispanic Heritage

The second part of this work focuses on programming for Hispanic youth.

Source: Immroth, B. F. and McCook, K. (2000) *Library Services to Youth of Hispanic Heritage*, Jefferson, NC: McFarland and Company.

Projects

Definition

A cooperative enterprise, often with a social or scientific purpose, but also in industry, etc. (OED)

Example

Kosoval Library Project 2000+

Aimed at 'the rehabilitation and enforcement of libraries in Kosova. The 3–4-year action plan both includes short-term projects and attempts to point out longer-term strategies for the recovery and development of library services'. One of its strategies, 'Libraries as offensive tools', has the aim 'not just to re-establish the situation of libraries in Kosova as it was before decay and destruction began in 1989. It is also to point out and recommend the use of libraries as offensive tools promoting values such as human rights, democracy, societal participation and cultural diversity and to stimulate the general flow of information and thus raising level[s] of knowledge.'

Source: Frederiksen, C. and Bakken, F. (2000) 'Libraries in Kosova/ Kosovo: A general assessment and a short and medium-term development plan'. IFLA/FAIFE. Available at: *http://www.ifla.org/faife/ faife/kosova/kosorepo.htm* (accessed 8 November 2006).

Protests

See also Rallies

Definition

The expressing of dissent from, or rejection of, the prevailing social, political, or cultural mores. (OED)

Example

IFLA protests closure of British Council Library in Zimbabwe

'The International Federation of Library Associations and Institutions (IFLA) has protested to His Excellency Mr Robert Mugabe, President of the Republic of Zimbabwe about the closure of the British Council Library and Information Service in Harare on 8 May 2001 and until further notice. Mr Alex Byrne, Chair of the IFLA Committee on Free Access to Information and Freedom of Expression, said "Librarians around the world are dismayed to learn of the closure of the British Council library service in Harare as a result of intimidation. We understand that this is part of a pattern of intimidation of international non-governmental organisations. The security of the premises no longer allow the staff to safely carry out their daily duties in a satisfactory manner, nor can it guarantee free and unhampered passage for the clients." The consequence of the closure of a facility such as the British Council Library will deny a great number of citizens of Zimbabwe free access to information and to the services normally provided by the Library for an indefinite and, we fear, long period of time. Mr Byrne noted "*It removes a facility which has been of tremendous educational, social and economic benefit to Zimbabwe for many years*". Contacts: Mr Alex Byrne, Chair, IFLA Committee on Free Access to Information and Freedom of Expression, Sydney, Australia. Ms Susanne Seidelin,

Director, IFLA FAIFE Office, Copenhagen, Denmark.'

Source: IFLA (2001) 'IFLA protests closure of British Council Library in Zimbabwe'. Available at: *http://www.ifla.org/V/press/pr05-21.htm* (accessed 26 October 2006).

Public forums

Definition

Forum: The public place or marketplace of a city. In ancient Rome the place of assembly for judicial and other public business. The place of public discussion; hence *fig.* (OED)

Public: That is open to, may be used by, or may or must be shared by, all members of the community. (OED)

Example

Vancouver Public Library's 'Speak Up' series

The series 'explores the fundamental question of *Who Owns Knowledge*'. The series provides a forum to 'speak up' on some of the most important issues facing today's world. 'Held at library branches across the city, Vancouver Public Library's *Speak Up* series will explore and discuss what you think about the ownership of genes, copyright, cost of drugs, selling universities and the value of Open Source and Open Access information technology. From October 24 to October 29, explore these crucial questions and share your vision for a better world. In a time of unrivalled growth of knowledge and scientific achievement "Who Owns Knowledge?" is one of the most important questions of the century. Should the essence of life, our genetic structure, be owned by anyone? What drives the drug industry? Do corporate sponsorships influence the development of new knowledge? These issues seriously affect the cost and quality of your health care, access to information, education and your future. *Speak Up* brings together many voices, perspectives and experiences and encourages public dialogue on important issues. This is an opportunity to share your point of view, to listen to others and to develop solutions to community concerns. In this series, VPL is inviting the public to join an open and frank dialogue on topics such as: When Is There Too Much Copyright? (October 24 and 26; 7:30–9 pm); Open or Closed: Software and Information (October 24 and 25; 7:30–9 pm); Selling Universities (October 26 and 28; 7:30–9 pm); Who Owns Your Genes? (October 25 and 27; 7:30–9 pm); Drugs for Profit or Health? (October 25 and 27; 7:30–9 pm); Who Owns Knowledge? (October 29; all day session from 9:30 am to 4:30 pm). The events are free and all are welcome.'

Source: Library News (2005) 'Vancouver Public Library's *Speak Up* series explores the fundamental question of *who owns knowledge*'. Available at: *http://www.vpl.ca/MDC/news05/speakup.html* (accessed 26 October 2006).

Publications

Definition

A work capable of being read or otherwise perceived (book, audio recording, video recording, CD-ROM, etc.), issued by a publisher for sale to the general public, usually in multiple copies and sometimes in multiple editions. (ODLIS)

Examples

InterActions: UCLA Journal of Education and Information Studies

'A peer-reviewed journal committed to the promotion of scholarship that examines education and information studies through interdisciplinary and critical perspectives. The journal seeks to link diverse theoretical and practical projects, as well as to provide a space for the voices of emerging scholars, activists and practitioners. Furthermore, as practitioners, researchers and institutions in education and information studies continue to face challenging times, we seek to promote alternative and liberatory visions, methodologies and practices. Of particular interest is work that analyzes inequities and links research to larger social and political contexts. Submissions may draw upon traditional areas of inquiry in these fields (e.g. policy, sociology, information-seeking and retrieval, pedagogy, history, psychological development, etc.) or provide insight from diverse disciplines (e.g. ethnic studies, literary criticism, political science, film, women's studies, technology studies, etc.). Submissions that utilize critical frameworks in provocative and politically engaged ways are encouraged; these frameworks may include, *but are not restricted to*, feminism, critical race theory, Marxism, postcolonialism, critical pedagogy, queer studies, disability studies, cultural studies, poststructuralism, etc. Regardless of the theoretical approach taken, submissions should advance current analyses and research in progressive directions.'

Source: *InterActions* 'Aims and scope'. Available at: *http://repositories .cdlib.org/gseis/interactions/aimsandscope.html* (accessed 26 October 2006).

An introduction to librarianship for human rights

Toni Samek's paper 'An introduction to librarianship for human rights', which she delivered at the Shared Dialogue and Learning: Educating for Human Rights and Global Citizenship Conference (University of Alberta, 11–13 November 2004), is part of the post-conference Human Rights Reader project. Samek's library-based contribution to this text provides an important opportunity for teachers in training to reconceptualise their understanding of the role of the library and the librarian in society.

Source: Samek, T. (2007, in press) 'An introduction to librarianship for human rights', in *The Human Rights Reader*, Buffalo, NY: SUNY Press.

Publishing

See Publications

Rallies

See also Protests

Definition

A political mass-meeting. Also, a mass-meeting of the supporters of any specified cause. (OED)

Example

Shout out to radical library workers

'Calling all radical library workers! Shout Out to radical library workers! Library workers are launching a project in support of the demonstrations surrounding the Republican National Convention in New York City August 29 to September 2, 2004. We will offer blog, chat, street and news reference, responding to questions from demonstrators. Sound ambitious? It is, so we need help. Please contact *info@radicalreference.info* if you would like to: answer e-mail reference questions; use your foreign language skills to answer questions and make the site more accessible; perform chat reference; participate in street reference; be a news librarian, teaching and researching for independent media journalists; help with the website; gather "Quick Facts and Contacts" info for street reference; rally together as library workers at the protests; send us money (for hats to identify us, materials, technical costs). All will be welcome to participate regardless of skill level or proximity to NYC. Indicate in your message in which areas you will participate.'

Source: *http://radicalreference.info/node/2* (accessed 8 November 2006).

Reaffirmations

Definition

Renewed affirmation; reassertion. (OED)

Example

ALA resolution reaffirming the principles of intellectual freedom in the aftermath of terrorist attacks

'WHEREAS: Benjamin Franklin counseled this nation: "They that can give up essential liberty to obtain a little temporary safety deserve neither liberty nor safety"; and WHEREAS: "The American Library Association believes that freedom of expression is an inalienable human right, necessary to self-government, vital to the resistance of oppression and crucial to the cause of justice and further, that the principles of freedom of expression should be applied by libraries and librarians throughout the world" (Policy 53.1.12, "*Universal Right to Free Expression*"); now, THEREFORE BE IT RESOLVED: that the American Library Association reaffirms the following principles and:

- Actively promotes dissemination of true and timely information necessary to the people in the exercise of their rights (Policy 53.8, "*Libraries: An American Value*");

- Opposes government censorship of news media and suppression of access to unclassified government information (Policy 53.3, "*Freedom to Read*"; Policy 53.5, "*Shield Laws*");

- Upholds a professional ethic of facilitating access to information, not monitoring access (Policy 53.1, "*Library Bill of Rights*"; Policy 53.1.17, "*Intellectual Freedom Principles for Academic Libraries*");

- Encourages libraries and their staff to protect the privacy and confidentiality of the people's lawful use of the library, its equipment and its resources (Policy 52.4, "*Policy on Confidentiality of Library Records*");

- Affirms that tolerance of dissent is the hallmark of a free and democratic society (Policy 53.1.12, "*Universal Right to Free Expression*");

- Opposes the misuse of governmental power to intimidate, suppress, coerce, or compel speech (Policy 53.4, "*Policy on Governmental Intimidation*"; Policy 53.6, "*Loyalty Oaths*");

and, BE IT FURTHER RESOLVED: that this resolution be forwarded to the President of the United States, to the Attorney General of the United States and to both Houses of Congress. Adopted by the ALA Council, January 23, 2002.'

Source: *http://www.ala.org/ala/oif/statementspols/ifresolutions/resolutionreaffirming.htm* (accessed 8 November 2006).

Representation

Definition

The fact of standing for, or in place of, some other thing or person, esp. with a right or authority to act on their account; substitution of one thing or person for another. (OED)

Example

John Pateman's representation on and leadership in groups working for social exclusion, internationalism and libraries as an agent of social change

'John Pateman has worked in public libraries for 27 years in six local authorities. He has been Head of Libraries in Hackney, Merton and Lincolnshire [UK]. He is particularly interested in social exclusion, internationalism and libraries as an agent of social change. He was a member of the government working group which produced *Libraries for All: Social Inclusion in Public Libraries* (1999) and of the research team which produced *Open to All? The Public Library and Social Exclusion* (2000). He was Head of Libraries in Merton when it won the Libraries Change Lives Award (2001) for services to asylum seekers and refugees. He was a member of the CILIP [Chartered Institute of Library and Information Professionals] Policy Action Group on Social Exclusion which produced *Making a Difference – Innovation and Diversity* (2002). He has written a publication on *Developing a Needs Based Library Service* (2003) as part of the NIACE Lifelines in adult learning series. He was a founding member of The Network, tackling social exclusion in libraries, museums, archives and galleries. He was a founding member of the Quality Leaders Programme for Black Library Workers. He is founder and co-editor of *Information for Social Change* and founder of the Cuban Libraries Solidarity Group. In 2002 he received the National Culture Award from the Cuban government for his services to Cuban libraries. In 2003 he shared a platform with Fidel Castro at the International Congress of Culture and Development in Havana. In 2004 he attended the World Gathering of Intellectuals and Artists in Defence of Humanity which was held in Caracas, Venezuela. In 2005 he gave two keynote addresses at the Vancouver Public Library staff conference. He is International Officer for the Lincolnshire branch of UNISON and he is secretary of the Lincolnshire Cuba Solidarity Campaign. He is a Fellow of CILIP and of the Institute of Public Sector Management. He is a committee member of the CILIP Diversity Group. He has written many articles on aspects of social exclusion – especially social class – community development and libraries in Cuba.'

Source: *http://www.libr.org/ISC/profile.html#a* (accessed 8 November 2006).

Resolutions

Definition

Refers to a formal statement of opinion or intention, issued by an assembly, organisation, or group. (ODLIS)

Examples

ALA resolution on workplace speech

'WHEREAS, The American Library Association is firmly committed to freedom of expression (Policy 53.1.12); and WHEREAS, The library is an institution that welcomes and promotes the expression of all points of view; and WHEREAS, Library staff are uniquely positioned to provide guidance on library policy issues that is informed by their experience and education; now, therefore, be it RESOLVED, That ALA Council amends Policy 54 (Library Personnel Practices) by adding:

> 54.21 Workplace Speech – Libraries should encourage discussion among library workers, including library administrators, of non-confidential professional and policy matters about the operation of the library and matters of public concern within the framework of applicable laws.

Adopted by the Council of the American Library Association. Sunday, June 26, 2005. In Chicago, Illinois.'

Source: *www.ala.org/ala/ourassociation/governanceb/council/councilagendas/annual2005a/CD38_1.doc* (accessed 8 November 2006).

Resolution on freedom of expression, censorship and libraries, adopted by the 55th IFLA Council and General Conference, 1989

'*Recalling* its resolution adopted in Munich in 1983 on behalf of librarians who are victims of violation of human rights and, *Whereas* Article 19 of the Universal Declaration of Human Rights (1948) proclaims that: "Everyone has the right to freedom of opinion and expression: includes freedom to hold opinions without interference and to seek, receive and impart information and ideas through any media and regardless of frontiers" and is recognized as an uncontested principle of international customary law, that all States, particularly members of the United Nations, must respect and *Whereas* respect of these freedoms is guaranteed, especially by the relevant concepts, which are enforceable, of the International Covenant of Civil and Political Rights (1966) of the United Nations (article 19) of universal applicability and also by regional treaties: the European Convention for the Protection of Human Rights and Fundamental Freedoms (1950), article 10; The American Convention on Human Rights (1969), article 13; the African Charter on Human and Peoples' Rights (1981), article 9; and reaffirmed by the Final Act of the Helsinki Conference (1975), chapter 1 a VII; text signed or ratified by a large majority of the States of the world; and *Whereas* librarians are particularly well informed about attempts to censor ideas and information which may effect them directly and as information on censorship must be represented at the international level when national recourse is impossible, illusory or failing to provide positive results, in a reasonable time; *Encourages* librarians and their associations globally to support the enforcement of Article 19 of the Universal Declaration of Human Rights, to exchange information on the abuse of restrictions of freedom of expression which concern them and, when necessary, to refer the matter to the President of IFLA and if applicable to other competent international organizations, non-governmental or intergovernmental; *Instructs* the President of IFLA, when such problem is legitimately and correctly submitted to him and after having studied and certified the data, when possible, to intervene in the most appropriate way with relevant authorities about freedom of expression and to cooperate, if necessary and to this end, with other international organizations.'

Source: *http://www.ifla.org/faife/policy/paris_e.htm* (accessed 8 November 2006).

Resource sharing

Definition

The activities that result from an agreement, formal or informal, among a group of libraries (usually a consortium or network) to share collections, data, facilities, personnel, etc., for the benefit of their users and to reduce the expense of collection development.

Example

Iraqi Libraries Network

'This site contains information related to the Iraqi libraries and may be used by librarians over the whole country. The main goal of the present web site is to rehabilitate library services in Iraq. Digital library with its main advanced features are to be made available in this site together with other facilities such as training for librarians, information about Iraqi libraries, statistics, reports, news and some other useful library and information services. This site has been created by Iraqi librarians for Iraqi librarians in an effort to help the Iraqi academic and scientific community. It has been a truly collaborative process together with the Goethe Institut (Germany's cultural institution), Bielefeld University Library (in Germany), Library and Information International (BII) and some other partners. A great achievement on the way to financial support and supply of the most important electronically based articles such as e-journal, e-books and other library materials! Further steps are to be followed later concerning the digitisation of some important collections in Iraqi libraries to make them available to different users.'

Source: *http://iraklib.ub.uni-bielefeld.de/index.html* (accessed 8 November 2006).

Responsible naming

See Naming, responsible

Round tables

Definition

In modern usage, a group established to discuss on an ongoing basis a range of topics and/or issues of concern to its members, usually within the context of a larger organisation. The original 'Round Table' preserved at Winchester, England, is believed to have been the centre around which the King Arthur of medieval legend met with his knights, its shape intended to prevent quarrels over precedence. (ODLIS)

Example

ALA's GLBT (gay, lesbian, bisexual and transgendered) round table

'The GLBTRT is a unit of the American Library Association. The GLBTRT was founded in 1970 as the Task Force on Gay Liberation. We are the nation's first gay, lesbian bisexual professional organization.'

Source: *http://www.ala.org/ala/glbtrt/welcomeglbtround.htm* (accessed 8 November 2006).

Scholarships

Definition

An award of access to an institution or a financial aid award for an individual (a 'scholar') for the purposes of furthering their education. A scholarship may be awarded based on range of criteria, which usually reflect the views or purposes of the donor or founder of the award. (Wikipedia)

Examples

Special Libraries Association's Affirmative Action Scholarship

'The Affirmative Action Scholarship will be granted only for graduate study in librarianship leading to a master's degree at a recognized school of library or information science. One $6,000 Affirmative Action Scholarship is available each year. The scholarship winner is notified in May. The official announcement and the presentation of the award will be made at the Association's Annual Conference in June.'

Source: *http://www.sla.org/content/learn/scholarship/sch-index/ #aaschola* (accessed 8 November 2006).

E. J. Josey Scholarship Award, sponsored by the Black Caucus of the American Library Association

'A noted administrator, author, educator, leader, librarian and scholar, Josey has been a life-long advocate for civil rights, human rights and equal opportunity for librarians of color, as well as a mentor to librarians of all races and ethnic backgrounds. Recognized as the founder of the Black Caucus of the ALA, he has been a champion for the eradication of racial bias from library systems and professional organizations throughout his career ... The E. J. Josey Scholarship Committee is happy to announce the topic for the 2006 Award competition. The 2006 theme is: "Over the past year, United States citizens have witnessed horrendous destruction in the Gulf States region. Hurricane Katrina and its aftermath disproportionately affected African Americans. Library services, as well as other information services, were either severely affected or completely eliminated. In an effort to recover from such tremendous loss, what aid and assistance, if any, do you feel librarians and in particular the African American librarian, can provide to these communities and individuals?" The E. J. Josey Scholarships are two (2) unrestricted grants of $2,000 (beginning in 1997) to be awarded annually to African American students enrolled in, or accepted by, ALA accredited programs. Applicants are judged on the basis of application essays of 1,000 to 1,200 words discussing issues, problems, or challenges facing library service to minority populations such as African Americans and other supporting documentation submitted for review by the scholarship committee. Persons wishing to apply must: Be an African American Citizen of the United States or Canada. Be enrolled or accepted by ALA-accredited graduate program leading to a degree in library and information science at the time of application. Submit an essay of 1,000–1,200 words discussing the theme.'

Source: *http://www.bcala.org/awards/josey.htm* (accessed 8 November 2006).

School libraries, alternative

Definition

School library: A library in a public or private elementary or secondary school that serves the information needs of its students and the curriculum needs of its teachers and staff. (ODLIS)

Alternative: Of two things; such that one or the other may be chosen, the choice of either involving the rejection of the other (sometimes of more than two). (OED)

Example

The People's Free Space Free School lending library, Portland, ME

'The People's Free Space Free School provides an open educational format that is committed to making education available to people free of charge. Since October 2002, The Free School has provided free workshops each month to the Portland community on a variety of topics …

We operate a lending library with over a thousand books and magazines. We try to stock titles that are not often found in other libraries and book stores including books on: political theory, sustainability, do-it-yourself skills, ecology, anarchy, radical history, indigenous issues, globalization and more.

TUG – the technology users group has set up an online database for all our Lending Library media. Here you have easy access to all titles of books, movies, zines and more…

The online database only has about a hundred of the thousands of items we have in our library. Volunteers have been coming in every Sunday to help input our catalog into the computer system and we can always use more help. If you're interested, just show up.'

Source: *http://www.peoplesfreespace.org/index.php?option=com_content&task=view&id=9&Itemid=14* (accessed 8 November 2006).

Security, humane

Definition

Humane: Marked by sympathy with and consideration for the needs and distresses of others; feeling or showing compassion and tenderness towards human beings and the lower animals; kind, benevolent. (OED)

Security: In the operation of libraries and archives, a general term encompassing all the equipment, personnel, practices and procedures used to prevent the theft or destruction of materials and equipment and to protect patrons and employees from the harmful actions of persons intent on mischief. (ODLIS)

Example

Joint UNESCO, CoE and IFLA/FAIFE Kosova Library Mission

'The UN Security Council Resolution 1244 entrusts the United Nations Mission in Kosova (UNMIK) with "performing basic civilian administrative functions" and "organising and overseeing the development of provisional institutions for democratic and autonomous self governance" in Kosova. In order to prepare an assessment of the situation concerning libraries and to establish rehabilitation guidelines UNESCO, the Council of Europe (CoE) and IFLA/FAIFE organised an expert mission to the main cities of Kosova. In the period from February 25th to March 7th, Mr Carsten Frederiksen, Deputy director of the IFLA/FAIFE Office in Copenhagen, Denmark and Mr Frode Bakken, President of the Norwegian Library Association, visited libraries in all major regions of Kosova. IFLA (International Federation of Library Association and Institutions) is concerned with the role of libraries in building and sustaining democracy.'

Source: Frederiksen, C. and Bakken, F. (2000) 'Libraries in Kosova/Kosovo: A general assessment and a short and medium-term development plan', IFLA/FAIFE. Available at: *http://www.ifla.org/faife/faife/kosova/kosorepo.htm* (accessed 8 November 2006).

Socially responsible investing

See Investing, socially responsible

Seminars

See also Education, LIS; Ethics training *and* Professional development

Definition

A class that meets for systematic study under the direction of a teacher. (OED)

Example

Library History Seminar XI: Libraries in Times of War, Revolution and Social Change

'The theme chosen for the conference, Libraries in Times of War, Revolution and Social Change, is a particularly timely one in terms of recent history. Events such as the pillage and burning of Iraq's National Library in Spring of 2003 have sent cultural shockwaves around the world. The apparent contradictions of libraries, traditionally taken to represent stability and continuity and wars and revolutions, which involve rapid and disruptive change, suggest a number of urgent historical questions.

Relevant topics, issues and concerns include: books and libraries as agents of cultural memory to be protected, appropriated or obliterated; library and archival collections and services as instruments of political power in providing, restricting or withholding access to information; libraries and their contents as cultural heritage and as booty; libraries as places of refuge, solace and practical help in times of war, revolution and social disruption; the responsibilities of the international community in creating and enforcing policies and procedures for the protection, recovery and repatriation of cultural artifacts, including books and libraries.

Paper sessions featuring scholars from seven countries will focus on the histories of library collections and services in the context of particular conflicts, populations, eras and geographic locations. Keynote speakers from North and South America, Europe and Asia will examine and discuss historical and contemporary libraries in times of social crisis and violent dislocation. What happens in such times to an institution that symbolizes and facilitates intellectual, social and cultural continuity? This approach offers a new kind of lens – and focus – for artifacts and events of the past that have heretofore been disregarded, minimized, or met with deliberate silence. The international scholarship presented at Library History Seminar XI represents an important step toward making this knowledge available to a wider audience.'

Source: Library History Seminar XI: Libraries in Times of War, Revolution and Social Change, 27–30 October 2005, University of Illinois at Urbana-Champaign. Available at: *http://conferences.lis .uiuc.edu/LHS.XI/home.html* (accessed 8 November 2006).

African seminar launched in Grahamstown

'A seminar to bring new developments and trends in services to blind and visually handicapped Africans began with a welcome from the Mayor Ms Nonthuthu Faku on Tuesday, February 16, 1999 at the Settler's Monument in Grahamstown. Ms Nonthuthu Faku spoke of the importance of the work of providing library services for the blind and bringing dignity and opportunity to those who are handicapped. The seminar, developed for libraries in English speaking Africa, was an IFLA project coordinated and developed by the South African Library for the Blind in Grahamstown. Dr William Rowland, Executive Director of the South African National Council for the Blind (and Chair of the South African Library for the Blind) opened the seminar on Wednesday, February 17, 1999 with an overview of conditions in South Africa. Ms Beatrice Christensen Sköld, Chair IFLA Section of Libraries for the Blind emphasized the importance of national and international cooperation in building good library services for blind people everywhere. The seminar brought together professionals from Africa and abroad to share their experiences and vision in providing library services to blind Africans. The impact of new technologies and directions were presented by speakers from the United Kingdom, Canada, Denmark, Sweden and Africa. Speakers from Zambia, Zimbabwe, South Africa, Uganda, Botswana, Swaziland, Uganda, Kenya and South Africa described the challenges faced by libraries for the Blind in Africa.'

Source: *http://www.ifla.org/VII/s31/nws1/spring99.htm* (accessed 8 November 2006).

Space, autonomous

Definitions

Space: A certain stretch, extent, or area of ground, surface, sky, etc.; an expanse. (OED)

Autonomous: Possessed of autonomy, self-governing, independent. (OED)

Example

Classism in the stacks: Libraries and poor people

'In Salt Lake City, Utah, a *Deseret News* report claims that "especially during the day, the library is filled with the homeless, who sometimes bother other library patrons with their odor, intoxication, or noise level. And while librarians stress they don't want to ban the homeless from the building, they also don't want leery residents to be fearful of enjoying the city's pristine new library. In search of a solution, the city library system is launching a new civility campaign designed to teach the homeless, children and others how to behave while in the library" ... In Houston, Texas, the City Council passed a series of new library regulations that prohibit "sleeping on tables, eating packaged food, using rest rooms for bathing and offensive bodily hygiene that constitutes a nuisance to others." It also bans "large amounts of personal possessions". In Elgin, Illinois, on the four tables in the library concession room, a notice reads: "In consideration of all who may wish to use these tables, use is limited to one hour per day". There is no 24-hour shelter where homeless people can gather in Elgin ... As an editorial gloss to this dismal litany: how can an ALA official proclaim "body odor" an enormous problem when the director of the San Luis Obispo Library himself has declared: "In 12 years, I can think of less than half a dozen incidents where people smell so bad that you can't get within ten feet of them"? And in calculating "enormity", isn't homelessness itself an "enormous problem", perhaps greater even than body odor? So, returning to my main theme: Why this pronounced failure to adopt and promote ALA's Poor People's Policy? Why the rush to further burden and even criminalize people who already have next to nothing and certainly don't enjoy a level playing field? Why the cascading efforts to exclude them from public spaces, deny them fair access to library resources and treat them as "problems", as pariahs? ... The hostility – or at least lack of sympathy – toward low-income people manifests in various barriers and kinds of discrimination. All together, the prejudice and what flows from it – the belief and the acts – can be called "classism": favoring one class over another, valuing middle and upper classes more highly than people at or below the poverty level. If librarians and others can first recognize their own attitudinal hang-ups, understanding what makes them view welfare mothers and homeless people, for example, unfavorably and ultimately grasping that poverty – not poor people – is the problem, that poverty can be reduced if not ended and that the most vulnerable and dispossessed among us are citizens and neighbors who deserve compassion, support and respect – if we can do these things in our heads and hearts, then there's a real chance to overcome classism.'

Source: Berman, S. (2005) 'Classism in the stacks', Jean E. Coleman Library Outreach Lecture. Available at: *http://www.ala.org/ala/olos/olosprograms/jeanecoleman/jeanecoleman.htm* (accessed 8 November 2006).

Speeches

Definition

An address or discourse of a more or less formal character delivered to an audience or assembly; an oration; also, the manuscript or printed copy or report of this. (OED)

Example

Why being a librarian is a radical choice

'When I look out at this room I see people who represent values that are distinctly different from the ones that currently govern the globe. These values are, in no particular order: Knowledge (as opposed to mere information gathering); Public Space (as opposed to commercial or private space); and Sharing (as opposed to buying and selling). It so happens that those are three of the most endangered and embattled values you could have chosen to represent. If you decided to represent "profit" or "global competitiveness" your lives would be easy. But you didn't and the very notion that that some things that are so important that cannot be fully owned and contained is under siege around the world.'

Source: Klein, N. (2003) 'Why being a librarian is a radical choice', Speech at the 2003 Joint American Library Association/Canadian Library Association Conference, 24 June, Toronto. Available at: *http://www.dissidentvoice.org/Articles7/Klein_Librarian.htm* (accessed 8 November 2006).

Storefronts

Definition

Of, pertaining to, or designating legal aid or citizen's advice organisations that operate from shop premises in order to be easily accessible. (OED)

Example

Biblioteca Anarchista Alberto Ghiraldo, Rosario, Argentina

'There are few workers' libraries preserving the history of the revolutionary Anarchist movement. Those that do exist in other countries often face problems far greater than ours, for instance the "Alberto Ghiraldo" Library in Rosario (The Argentine). The library, with priceless records and memories of workers' risings in Patagonia and

Buenos Aires, with all that means for the future. With the Centro de Estudios Sociales "Rafael Barrett" and other anarcho-syndicalist and anarcho-ecological groups, they have had to move again as the result of economic problems, the same as have caused the Kate Sharpley Library to be prevented from developing in the first years of its existence. Now they are working to deal with present needs and acquiring their own building, as we are.'

Source: *http://flag.blackened.net/ksl/bullet2.htm#Argentinean% 20Library* (accessed 8 November 2006).

Student engagement

Definition

Engagement: The state of being engaged in fight; a battle, conflict, encounter; also formerly, a single combat. (OED)

Example

Future Librarians for Intellectual Freedom

Future Librarians for Intellectual Freedom (FLIF) is a student group at the School of Library and Information Studies, University of Alberta. FLIF is 'committed to promoting intellectual freedom and social responsibility both within the school and throughout the University of Alberta community. [In its] inaugural year (2004/2005) ... FLIF was able to circulate within the University community and spread the word about intellectual freedom and social responsibility and also raise the profile of the library school and of future librarians ... FLIF also headed out on campus in the spring, celebrating *Freedom to Read Week* by promoting the awareness of challenged books. Taking a cue from the *Freedom to Read Week* website, FLIF decided to take part in the Bookcrossing campaign by randomly distributing challenged books in public places on campus. Bookcrossing labels were attached to the books that provided a short explanation about challenged books and freedom of expression while inviting the finder of the book to visit the Bookcrossing website. There they could register the book as "found" as well as discover more information about challenged books. In addition, FLIF set up an information table in the Students' Union Building to raise awareness of the Bookcrossing campaign and intellectual freedom. This campaign turned out to be very successful and of the 26 books released so far, six have been caught and registered by their founders, which is on par with the national Bookcrossing catch and release rate. Intellectual freedom and social responsibility were promoted within the school as well, the most impressive project being a school art show.'

Source: Thomson, V. (2004) 'Future Librarians for Intellectual Freedom (FLIF): a student initiative', *School Libraries in Canada: A Journal of the Canadian Association for School Libraries* 24(4). Available from: *http://www.schoollibraries.ca/articles/159.aspx* (accessed 6 July 2006).

Student groups

See Student engagement

Symposiums

See also Forums

Definition

A meeting or conference for discussion of some subject; hence, a collection of opinions delivered, or a series of articles contributed, by a number of persons on some special topic. (OED)

Example

Localizing the Internet: ethical issues in intercultural perspective

'The ongoing debate on the impact of the Internet at a global and local level is at the core of today's and tomorrow's political decision-making, particularly in a world that turns more and more unified – and divided. It is also at the core of academic research on what has been called

Information Ethics. The leading ethical question is how embodied human life is possible within local cultural traditions and the horizon of a global digital environment. The first international symposium of the International Center for Information Ethics (ICIE) will deal with this question from three perspectives:

- Internet for Social and Political Development: Community Building
- Internet for Cultural Development: Restructuring the Media
- Internet for Economic Development: Empowering the People

The ethical perspective on intercultural aspects of the global digital network is a normative as well as a formative one. The symposium addresses the question of how people with different cultural backgrounds integrate the Internet in their lives. This concerns in the first place community building. How far does the Internet affect, for better or worse, local community building? How far does it allow democratic consultation? How do people construct their lives within this medium? How does it affect their customs, languages and everyday problems? The question about information justice is thus not just an issue of giving everybody access to the global network (a utopian goal?), but rather an issue on how the digital network helps people to better manage their lives while avoiding the dangers of exploitation and discrimination.

It deals, secondly, with the changes produced by the Internet on traditional media, such as oral and written customs, newspapers, radio and TV, the merger of mass media, the telephone and the internet and the impact of the Internet on literary culture. The symposium also reflects on the next generation of information and communication technologies such as ubiquitous computing and on what might be called the post-internet era. This aspect of the ethical question focuses on new methods of manipulation and control made possible or aggravated by the Internet.

Finally, it deals with the economic impact of the Net. Is it a medium that helps people to better opportunities for economic development? Or is it an instrument of oppression and colonialism? What is the impact of this technology on the environment? How does it affect what has been called cultural memory or cultural sustainability?'

Source: International Center for Information Ethics (2004) 'Localizing the Internet: ethical issues in intercultural perspective', International ICIE Symposium, 4–6 October, Karlsruhe. Available at: *http://icie .zkm.de/congress2004* (accessed 26 October 2006).

Teaching

Definition

Showing the way; direction, guidance. (OED)

Example

Scales, P. (2001) Teaching Banned Books: 12 Guides for Young Readers, Chicago: American Library Association

'Veteran school librarian Pat Scales, who wrote "Teaching Banned Books: 12 Guides for Young Readers" and is a member of the American Library Association's Intellectual Freedom Committee, suggests that banned books have important lessons to teach youth, particularly when they are guided by their parents. These books can help to: Spark open and honest discussion; Understand and debate real-life issues; Learn to function in a changing society; Nurture intellectual growth; Encourage creative and critical thinking; Recognize and accept cultural differences; Value literature of all genres. Parents, teachers and librarians can all help children to understand sometimes difficult or complex issues. Scales offers the following tips for parents sharing banned books with kids: Read the book together; Discuss the book with kids; Discuss why people are afraid for kids to read some books; Talk about the specific reasons that people give for banning the book; Talk about the importance of reading the entire book before forming an opinion; Encourage kids to ask questions; Ask kids to state their own opinions about the book.'

Source: *http://www.ala.org/ala/pio/piopresskits/bannedbooksweek2004/ bbwparenttips.htm* (accessed 8 November 2006).

Training, activist

Definitions

Training: Discipline and instruction directed to the development of powers or formation of character; education, rearing, bringing up;

systematic instruction and exercise in some art, profession, or occupation, with a view to proficiency in it.

Activism: A doctrine or policy of advocating energetic action. Hence *activist*, an advocate of activism in either sense. (OED)

Activism, in a general sense, can be described as intentional action to bring about social or political change. This action is in support of, or opposition to, one side of an often controversial argument. The word 'activism' is often used synonymously with protest or dissent, but activism can stem from any number of political orientations and take a wide range of forms, from writing letters to newspapers or politicians, political campaigning, economic activism (such as boycotts or preferentially patronising preferred businesses), rallies and street marches, strikes, or even guerrilla tactics. In the more confrontational cases, an activist may be called a freedom fighter by some and a terrorist by others, depending on whether the commentator supports the activist's ends. (Wikipedia)

Example

Training the trainers

The 'Training the trainers' workshop for librarians was held at the World Social Forum, 3–5 July 2006, Nairobi. It was organised by the Kenya Library Association with financial support from the Finnish Embassy. 'Shiraz Durrani from the London Metropolitan University and Mikael Böök from the Network Institute for Global Democratization (NIGD) gave sessions on globalisation and information and on the World Social Forum. Mary Wanjohi and Esther Obachi, both librarians at the university of Nairobi gave sessions on the information activist and on the the tasks of librarians in the WSF process. In addition, Mr Onyango Oloo from the WSF 2007 Organising Committee contributed a session on the preparations towards the Nairobi WSF (20–25 January 2007) and Ms Emma Lochery, a political economy graduate from Oxford, introduced the Tax Justice Network, which is now setting up its African branch. The participants in the workshop, ca 30 persons, were librarians from the Kenya National Library Service and various universities in Nairobi, Kisumu, Eldoret and Kikuyu. Two participants came from Kampala, Uganda.

The purpose of this workshop: Generally, participation in the WSF can be seen as a form of active citizenship, but the librarians also have a professional role to play in the WSF process. While the role of interpreters and translators in the WSF is to help speakers of different languages understand each other, and that of journalists is to spread the news from the WSF to their audiences, librarians should care for the documentation, preservation and presentation of the WSF over a longer period of time. The purpose of this workshop is thus to prepare and train librarians for participation in the World Social Forum 20–25 January 2007 and in the WSF process, both as citizens and in their role as information specialists. This particular workshop should also be useful for trainers, who will themselves prepare and train more librarians for participation in the WSF'. Module 1: Towards a relevant public library service in Africa; Module 2: The World Social Forum and the librarians of the world; Module 3: WSF documentation and information management.

Source: *http://www.nigd.org/libraries/bamako-nairobi/tot-workshop/* (accessed 8 November 2006).

Translations

Definition

A passage from a speech or written work, or an entire speech or work, put into the words of another language (e.g. English into Spanish) or into a more modern form of the same language (e.g. Old English or Middle English into contemporary English), usually to make the text more accessible to individuals who are unable to read it in the original language. (ODLIS)

Example

The German translation of the Declaration from Buenos Aires on Information, Documentation and Libraries: Alternative action programmes from Latin America for the information society

In February 2005, Akribie (Arbeitskreis kritischer BibliothekarInnen) the Working Group of Critical Librarians in Germany, published a German language translation of the Declaration from Buenos Aires on Information, Documentation and Libraries: Alternative action programmes from Latin America for the information society in their journal *BuB-Forum für Bibliothek und Information* (*http://www.b-u-b.de/0502/index.php?frame=inhalt*). This is the official journal of the German Library Association. Akribie subsequently presented this version at the German Library Congress (Bibliothekartag), Heinrich-Heine University, Düsseldorf, 15–18 March 2005.

Source: *http://72.14.253.104/search?q=cache:857tgb2TFV4J:www .inforosocial.org/german.html+the+German+Library+Congress+(Bibliot hekartag+2005),+which+was+held+from+March+15th+to+18th+at+Hei nrich-Heine+University+in+D%C3%BCsserldorf.&hl=en&gl=ca&ct= clnk&cd=1* (accessed 7 November 2006).

The abridged, English language edition of a book about independent public libraries by Anders Ericson, originally published in Norwegian

'The democratic potential of public libraries made me choose library education in 1973 and I've been engaged in democracy issues since then; I published a book on "the Independent Public Library" in 2001; in Norwegian only *http://wgate.bibsys.no/gate1/SHOW?objd= 012275174&lang=N*, but I wrote a short version in English for ISC: *http://www.libr.org/ISC/articles/18-Ericson-1.html*.'

Source: *http://www.libr.org/isc/profile.html#h* (accessed 7 November 2006).

Trustees, education of

Definition

Library Trustee: A member of an appointed or elected board responsible for overseeing the growth and development of a library or library system, including long-range planning and policymaking, public relations and fund-raising. Trustees are usually library advocates but may sometimes be political appointees. (ODLIS)

Note: For basic trustee roles and responsibilities, see the British Columbia Library Association's Trustee Handbook at *http://www.bclta .org/thbook.html* (accessed 8 November 2006).

Example

Toni Samek's address to the Vancouver Public Library Board and staff

In September 2005, Toni Samek delivered the keynote speech at the Vancouver Public Library (VPL) Board of Trustees Strategic Planning Workshop. The title of her talk was 'Libraries, Social Action and Neutrality'. Toni talked about re-stating the VPL vision in a way that moved it closer to a human rights orientation, especially in terms of the right to participate in the cultural life of the community. Toni subsequently participated in the two-day Board discussions to exchange ideas about how this might play out in both rhetoric and reality. Toni's invitation came from Brian Campbell of VPL management (Director, Systems and Special Projects) who had previously (spring 2005) invited John Pateman to speak to the VPL staff on the subject of needs-based library service. Seeking Board approval to move a library in non-traditional directions requires trustee (and staff) education, often from outside perspectives. In this case, Brian had been working informally inside the VPL system for some time in order to set the stage for more formal Board and staff discussions.

Websites

See also Wikis

Definition

A document or a set of linked documents, usually associated with a particular person, organisation or topic, that is held on such a computer system and can be accessed as part of the World Wide Web. (OED)

Example

Librarians Without Borders website

Librarians Without Borders' website provides an online base for news of its projects.

'Our philosophy

Librarians Without Borders (LWB) believes that access to information is vital in supporting learning and literacy, reducing poverty, empowering citizens and building healthy, strong communities. We envision a global society where all people have equal access to information resources.

Mission

Librarians Without Borders (LWB) is a non-profit organization that strives to improve access to information resources regardless of language, geography, or religion, by forming partnerships with community organizations in developing regions.

Vision

LWB envisions a global society where all people have equal access to information resources.

Values

LWB holds a core set of values that form the basis of our existence and steer our activities:

1. Libraries have a fundamental role as defenders of intellectual freedom and providers of equal access to information.
2. Access to information is vital in supporting learning and literacy, reducing poverty, empowering citizens and building healthy, strong communities.
3. We do not draw cultural or linguistic boundaries – diversity is embraced; we will work with our partners in their own cultural context and in their own languages.

4. Our efforts are enhanced by working collaboratively, internally as well as externally with the domestic and international community, to further our mutual goals.'

Source: *http://www.lwb-online.org/about/mission.html* (accessed 8 November 2006).

Wikis

Definition

A web application that allows users to add content to a collaborative hypertext web resource (co-authoring), as in an Internet forum and permits others to edit that content (open editing). Authorisations and passwords are not required and content can be changed by anyone simply by clicking on a 'edit' link located on the page. A wiki may have policies to govern editing and procedures for handling edit wars. Activity within the site can be watched and reviewed by any visitor to the site. The term also refers to the collaborative server software used to collectively create such a website, allowing web pages (stored in a database) to be easily created and updated. A prime example is Wikipedia. (ODLIS)

Example

Radical Reference Wiki

'The intention for the wiki is to have our very own collaborative workspace. The first project listed on RR wiki is the Alt travel guide to San Antonio (*http://wiki.radicalreference.info/index.php/Travel_guides*). I've started it, but need help from those who have visited, lived, know someone who lives in San Antonio, to flesh out the guide. I'd like to make this the parking spot for all future alternative travel guides to ALA cities. For those who are unsure about how wikis work, please see *http://meta .wikimedia.org/wiki/MediaWiki_User*'s_Guide. Wikis use html, but also their own shorthand for links, formatting and organizing pages.'

Source: *http://wiki.radicalreference.info/index.php/Main_Page* (accessed 8 November 2006).

Women, status of

Definition

Status: the legal standing or position of a person as determined by his membership of some class of persons legally enjoying certain rights or subject to certain limitations; condition in respect, e.g. of liberty or servitude, marriage or celibacy, infancy or majority. (OED)

Examples

Role of libraries in enhancing status of women in post-war societies: The case of Kosovo

'Below there are practical suggestions to be introduced to the Kosovo Ministry of Culture, Youth and Sports to improve the situation of women security with the use of libraries.

1. Invest attention and funds to the revival of the rural libraries, as those that have most outreach capacity for the population.

2. Spread the educational sources among libraries that discuss the concepts and experiences of violence directed on women in Kosovo and other places in the world. Spread information about the relief organization and remedies available for the victims.

3. Open legal corners to educate the population about their rights and the rights of women. Refer the population to the free legal practitioners working in the area.

4. Disseminate literature of the Kosovo writers, women and men to discuss the common experiences of people to establish the channels for communication between the groups of different ages and ethnic backgrounds. Spread the literature about experiences of women in similar situations – Bosnian, Chechen – for the locals to learn and apply their methods of survival. Open the literary centers and societies in the libraries.

5. Within the libraries equipped by modern ITs open the computer literacy courses and establish income generating and skill training projects for children and especially for young girls. Spread the educational sources such as a free database Mapping the World of Women Information via CD-ROMs wherever the Internet connection is non-available.'

Source: Popova-Gosart, U. (2005) 'Role of libraries in enhancing status of women in post-war societies: The case of Kosovo'. Available at: *http://www.ifla.org/IV/ifla71/papers/163ePopova-Gosart.pdf* (accessed 2 July 2006).

Greater Edmonton Library Association (GELA) and the Women's Reintegration Chaplaincy

'Join us for a one-hour talk about the Women's Reintegration Chaplaincy and the work they do to help women leaving Federal prison fit back into society. Through speaking engagements and workshops with service and professional groups like GELA, they provide first-hand information about the incarceration and parole experience. The hope is to bring community members closer to understanding the many challenges faced by women on parole, and encourage society to welcome them back to the community.' Date: February 1, 2007. Location: Centennial Room, Stanley Milner Public Library, Edmonton, Alberta. Free. 'GELA hopes to establish a women's prison sub-committee that could look at future volunteering, fundraising, or reintegration opportunities with the Edmonton Institute for Women and/or the Women's Reintegration Chaplaincy.' For more information about the Women's Reintegration Chaplaincy, see *http://www.e4calberta.org/wrc/info.html*. For information about the Edmonton Institution for Women, see *http://www.csccc.gc.ca/text/facilit/institutprofiles/edforwomen_e.shtml*.

Source: *http://www.gela.ca/* (accessed 12 January 2007).

Closing thought

In the coming years, it will be instructive to monitor UNESCO, IFLA, national libraries, library associations and their relationship to the critical library movement in its push for the development of a more humanistic profession grounded in an unfettered cultural record, the ability to publicly finance library work, freedom of expression on professional and policy issues within library ranks, respect for cultural diversity, desire to redress concessions, omissions, absences and negations in collective memory and progress in opposing commodification of information, 'corporate globalization, privatization of social services, monopolization of information resources, profit-driven destruction (or private appropriation and control) of cultural artifacts and the human record'.[1] A fundamental condition for realising this vision is the advancement of library and information studies programmes worldwide that demonstrate a concern for people and the amelioration of social problems. Like this author, progressive library educator Christine Pawley is hopeful on this count. She observes, hegemony 'is never complete and historically some librarians and library educators have resisted ideological domination'.[2] By way of example, this book is humbly conceived to support library and information workers' political and transformative struggle in a fragile world.

Notes

1. Rosenzweig, M. (2001) 'What progressive librarians believe: an international perspective,' *Innovation* 22 (June): 1–5
2. Pawley, C. (1998) 'Hegemony's handmaid? The library and information studies curriculum from a class perspective,' *Library Quarterly* 68(2): 123–44

Appendix

Resolution on behalf of librarians who are victims of violation of human rights

This resolution was submitted by the French National IFLA Commission on behalf of all French Association Members of IFLA, which also separately submitted the same motion (but in French only) with a covering letter. The English text was approved by the Council.

In the name of human rights, librarians must, as a profession, express their solidarity with those of their colleagues who are persecuted for their opinions, wherever they may be. The Council mandates the President of IFLA, when informed of specific cases, after due considerations to intervene when appropriate with competent authorities on behalf of these colleagues.

Resolution adopted by the 49th IFLA Council and General Conference in Munich, Germany, 1983.

IFLA resolution on freedom of expression, censorship and libraries

'The Council of the International Federation of Library Associations and Institutions (IFLA) meeting in Paris on 25 August 1989,

Recalling its resolution adopted in Munich in 1983 on behalf of librarians who are victims of violation of human rights and,

Whereas Article 19 of the Universal Declaration of Human Rights (1948) proclaims that: "Everyone has the right to freedom of opinion and expression: includes freedom to hold opinions without interference and to seek, receive and impart information and ideas through any media and regardless of frontiers", and is recognized as an uncontested principle of international customary law, that all States, particularly members of the United Nations, must respect, and

Whereas respect of these freedoms is guaranteed, especially by the relevant concepts, which are enforceable, of the International Covenant of Civil and Political Rights (1966) of the United Nations (article 19) of universal applicability, and also by regional treaties: the European Convention for the Protection of Human Rights and Fundamental Freedoms (1950), article 10; The American Convention on Human Rights (1969), article 13; the African Charter on Human and Peoples' Rights (1981), article 9; and reaffirmed by the Final Act of the Helsinki Conference (1975), chapter 1 a VII; text signed or ratified by a large majority of the States of the world; and

Whereas librarians are particularly well informed about attempts to censor ideas and information which may effect them directly, and as information on censorship must be represented at the international level when national recourse is impossible, illusory or failing to provide positive results, in a reasonable time;

Encourages librarians and their associations globally to support the enforcement of Article 19 of the Universal Declaration of Human Rights, to exchange information on the abuse of restrictions of freedom of expression which concern them and, when necessary, to refer the matter to the President of IFLA and if applicable to other competent international organizations, non-governmental or intergovernmental;

Instructs the President of IFLA, when such problem is legitimately and correctly submitted to him, and after having studied and certified the data, when possible, to intervene in the most appropriate way with relevant authorities about freedom of expression and to cooperate, if necessary and to this end, with other international organizations.'

Universal declaration of human rights

On 10 December 1948, the General Assembly of the United Nations adopted and proclaimed the Universal Declaration of Human Rights, the full text of which appears in the following pages. Following this historic act the Assembly called upon all member countries to publicise the text of the Declaration and 'to cause it to be disseminated, displayed, read and expounded principally in schools and other educational institutions, without distinction based on the political status of countries or territories.'

Preamble

Whereas recognition of the inherent dignity and of the equal and inalienable rights of all members of the human family is the foundation of freedom, justice and peace in the world,

Whereas disregard and contempt for human rights have resulted in barbarous acts which have outraged the conscience of mankind, and the advent of a world in which human beings shall enjoy freedom of speech and belief and freedom from fear and want has been proclaimed as the highest aspiration of the common people,

Whereas it is essential, if man is not to be compelled to have recourse, as a last resort, to rebellion against tyranny and oppression, that human rights should be protected by the rule of law,

Whereas it is essential to promote the development of friendly relations between nations,

Whereas the peoples of the United Nations have in the Charter reaffirmed their faith in fundamental human rights, in the dignity and worth of the human person and in the equal rights of men and women and have determined to promote social progress and better standards of life in larger freedom,

Whereas Member States have pledged themselves to achieve, in co-operation with the United Nations, the promotion of universal respect for and observance of human rights and fundamental freedoms,

Whereas a common understanding of these rights and freedoms is of the greatest importance for the full realization of this pledge,

Now, Therefore The General Assembly proclaims This Universal Declaration of Human Rights as a common standard of achievement for all peoples and all nations, to the end that every individual and every organ of society, keeping this Declaration constantly in mind, shall strive by teaching and education to promote respect for these rights and freedoms and by progressive measures, national and international, to secure their universal and effective recognition and observance, both among the peoples of Member States themselves and among the peoples of territories under their jurisdiction.

Article 1: All human beings are born free and equal in dignity and rights. They are endowed with reason and conscience and should act towards one another in a spirit of brotherhood.

Article 2: Everyone is entitled to all the rights and freedoms set forth in this Declaration, without distinction of any kind, such as race, colour, sex, language, religion, political or other opinion, national or social origin, property, birth or other status. Furthermore, no distinction shall be made on the basis of the political, jurisdictional or international status of the country or territory to which a person belongs, whether it be independent, trust, non-self-governing or under any other limitation of sovereignty.

Article 3: Everyone has the right to life, liberty and security of person.

Article 4: No one shall be held in slavery or servitude; slavery and the slave trade shall be prohibited in all their forms.

Article 5: No one shall be subjected to torture or to cruel, inhuman or degrading treatment or punishment.

Article 6: Everyone has the right to recognition everywhere as a person before the law.

Article 7: All are equal before the law and are entitled without any discrimination to equal protection of the law. All are entitled to equal protection against any discrimination in violation of this Declaration and against any incitement to such discrimination.

Article 8: Everyone has the right to an effective remedy by the competent national tribunals for acts violating the fundamental rights granted him by the constitution or by law.

Article 9: No one shall be subjected to arbitrary arrest, detention or exile.

Article 10: Everyone is entitled in full equality to a fair and public hearing by an independent and impartial tribunal, in the determination of his rights and obligations and of any criminal charge against him.

Article 11: (1) Everyone charged with a penal offence has the right to be presumed innocent until proved guilty according to law in a public trial at which he has had all the guarantees necessary for his defence. (2) No one shall be held guilty of any penal offence on account of any act or omission which did not constitute a penal offence, under national or international law, at the time when it was committed. Nor shall a heavier penalty be imposed than the one that was applicable at the time the penal offence was committed.

Article 12: No one shall be subjected to arbitrary interference with his privacy, family, home or correspondence, nor to attacks upon his honour and reputation. Everyone has the right to the protection of the law against such interference or attacks.

Article 13: (1) Everyone has the right to freedom of movement and residence within the borders of each state. (2) Everyone has the right to leave any country, including his own, and to return to his country.

Article 14: (1) Everyone has the right to seek and to enjoy in other countries asylum from persecution. (2) This right may not be invoked in the case of prosecutions genuinely arising from non-political crimes or from acts contrary to the purposes and principles of the United Nations.

Article 15: (1) Everyone has the right to a nationality. (2) No one shall be arbitrarily deprived of his nationality nor denied the right to change his nationality.

Article 16: (1) Men and women of full age, without any limitation due to race, nationality or religion, have the right to marry and to found a family. They are entitled to equal rights as to marriage, during marriage and at its dissolution. (2) Marriage shall be entered into only with the free and full consent of the intending spouses. (3) The family is the natural and fundamental group unit of society and is entitled to protection by society and the State.

Article 17: (1) Everyone has the right to own property alone as well as in association with others. (2) No one shall be arbitrarily deprived of his property.

Article 18: Everyone has the right to freedom of thought, conscience and religion; this right includes freedom to change his religion or belief, and freedom, either alone or in community with others and in public or private, to manifest his religion or belief in teaching, practice, worship and observance.

Article 19: Everyone has the right to freedom of opinion and expression; this right includes freedom to hold opinions without interference and to seek, receive and impart information and ideas through any media and regardless of frontiers.

Article 20: (1) Everyone has the right to freedom of peaceful assembly and association. (2) No one may be compelled to belong to an association.

Article 21: (1) Everyone has the right to take part in the government of his country, directly or through freely chosen representatives. (2) Everyone has the right of equal access to public service in his country. (3) The will of the people shall be the basis of the authority of government; this will shall be expressed in periodic and genuine elections which shall be by universal and equal suffrage and shall be held by secret vote or by equivalent free voting procedures.

Article 22: Everyone, as a member of society, has the right to social security and is entitled to realization, through national effort and international co-operation and in accordance with the organization and resources of each State, of the economic, social and cultural rights indispensable for his dignity and the free development of his personality.

Article 23: (1) Everyone has the right to work, to free choice of employment, to just and favourable conditions of work and to protection against unemployment. (2) Everyone, without any discrimination, has the right to equal pay for equal work. (3) Everyone who works has the right to just and favourable remuneration ensuring for himself and his family an existence worthy of human dignity, and supplemented, if necessary, by other means of social protection. (4) Everyone has the right to form and to join trade unions for the protection of his interests.

Article 24: Everyone has the right to rest and leisure, including reasonable limitation of working hours and periodic holidays with pay.

Article 25: (1) Everyone has the right to a standard of living adequate for the health and well-being of himself and of his family, including food, clothing, housing and medical care and necessary social services, and the right to security in the event of unemployment, sickness, disability, widowhood, old age or other lack of livelihood in circumstances beyond his control. (2) Motherhood and childhood are entitled to special care and assistance. All children, whether born in or out of wedlock, shall enjoy the same social protection.

Article 26: (1) Everyone has the right to education. Education shall be free, at least in the elementary and fundamental stages. Elementary education shall be compulsory. Technical and professional education shall be made generally available and higher education shall be equally accessible to all on the basis of merit. (2) Education shall be directed to the full development of the human personality and to the strengthening of respect for human rights and fundamental freedoms. It shall promote understanding, tolerance and friendship among all nations, racial or religious groups, and shall further the activities of the United Nations for the maintenance of peace. (3) Parents have a prior right to choose the kind of education that shall be given to their children.

Article 27: (1) Everyone has the right freely to participate in the cultural life of the community, to enjoy the arts and to share in scientific advancement and its benefits. (2) Everyone has the right to the protection of the moral and material interests resulting from any scientific, literary or artistic production of which he is the author.

Article 28: Everyone is entitled to a social and international order in which the rights and freedoms set forth in this Declaration can be fully realized.

Article 29: (1) Everyone has duties to the community in which alone the free and full development of his personality is possible. (2) In the exercise of his rights and freedoms, everyone shall be subject only to such limitations as are determined by law solely for the purpose of securing due recognition and respect for the rights and freedoms of others and of meeting the just requirements of morality, public order and the general welfare in a democratic society. (3) These rights and freedoms may in no case be exercised contrary to the purposes and principles of the United Nations.

Article 30: Nothing in this Declaration may be interpreted as implying for any State, group or person any right to engage in any activity or to perform any act aimed at the destruction of any of the rights and freedoms set forth herein.

Index

Printed in the United States
120450LV00002B/19/A

9 781843 341468